Magnificent
Obesity

Magnificent Obesity

My Search for Wellness,
Voice and Meaning
in the Second Half of Life

MARTHA M MORAVEC

Hatherleigh Press is committed to preserving and protecting the natural resources of the earth. Environmentally responsible and sustainable practices are embraced within the company's mission statement.

Visit us at www.hatherleighpress.com and register online for free offers, discounts, special events, and more.

Magnificent Obesity
Text copyright © 2014 Martha M Moravec

Library of Congress Cataloging-in-Publication Data is available upon request.
ISBN: 978-1-57826-505-3

Cover and Interior Design by Dede Cummings
Cover Image StockImageGroup/Thinkstock

Printed in the United States
10 9 8 7 6 5 4 3 2 1

Disclaimer:
Although she has not consciously taken liberties in her recollection of people, places and events, the author maintains that this is her story, subject to her memories, opinions, impressions and beliefs.

Contents

For my mother —

Nemesis

Hero

Friend

LITTLE MARTY

As I move toward a better understanding of my obesity, I am coaxed step by intricate step into a dance with four partners: anxiety, agnosticism, addictive behavior and aging. This is not a weight loss memoir. It is not a size acceptance manifesto. It is a portrait of obesity that regards fat as neither fabulous nor expendable until it can be fully comprehended and briefly called magnificent for its capacity to initiate new life.

ONE

She was afraid of her own bathtub.

She bathed every night in the depths of a large, double-ended roll rim claw-foot tub, a treasure to some; to her, a threat. It did not appear to be a reproduction, so it had to have been old, at least as old as the building she lived in, as old as the musty, sagging upstairs apartment that had housed her progressively thinning hair and bones for the past 25 years.

She craved the cascading heat of a shower, but the shower kit had been carelessly installed and the enclosure ring tended to shake loose with one rash pull on the curtains. Soaking in a hot tub was her sole means of hydrotherapy, drug-free relief for her exhausted joints.

Eucalyptus-scented bubbles often added to the sense of occasion, eucalyptus with hints of menthol and sage, or bubbles made of French lavender, white tea and calendula. These soft touches varied. On bubbleless nights, it could be Dr. Bronner's 18-in-1 Hemp Pure-Castile Peppermint Soap or drops of essential oils.

For illumination, a translucent beige night-light sufficed, occasionally enhanced by white candles. The room was ever and always dimly lit. For entertainment, Chopin Nocturnes alternated with a favorite movie on her iPad, a movie she had to have seen more than 20 times so she could afford to miss snatches of dialogue whenever the water slopped up around the tub's overflow plate.

Still, these amenities did not calm her fear of death.

The delights of her bath alternated with dread. The anticipation of easing down into a swirl of steam perfumed by sandalwood, ylang ylang, or rose came compromised by a sense of doom. Her image of herself disrobing like a nymph and dabbing her toes into a pool of water sweetened by organic extracts and herbal emollients did not purge her fear of death nor did it eliminate the prospect of untimely death overtaking her one night, one lonely, candlelit, sublimely scented night in her own bath.

She feared that the claw-foot tub would split open under her substantial weight. She imagined that the tub itself suffered from porous bones, which had grown more and more brittle over time and more liable to fracture, and that its floor, which had borne her 300 pounds for the past 10 years, would finally snap. She imagined the tub's floor cracking and buckling up into great shards of steel and fiberglass and cutting her clean in two.

Or perhaps it would not be so clean. Perhaps the porcelain would shatter into a dozen jagged edges and points, deadly weapons that took shape in her mind as railroad spikes or the heads of medieval maces, pasta forks and tongs, skate blades with toe picks and the runners on sleds. She would be hacked to pieces because she had achieved a bulk that even concrete or fiberglass or porcelain—or whatever the hell it was made of—could not support.

It would be bloodier than the death of Marat in his medicinal tub, when the assassin's 5-inch kitchen knife sliced into a carotid artery. It would be bloodier than Marion's shower at the Bates Motel, bloodier than the death of Frankie Pentangeli in The Godfather Part II, who opens his wrists, Roman-like, while surrendering to the anesthetic of his bath.

The downstairs neighbors and first responders would break open the door and find at their feet strips of pinkish bubbles rippling over an expanding pool of pink water. Inching closer, they would discover white chunks of tub strewn with puce-colored body parts, minced gut, and slabs of flesh.

They would not see, or even think to look for, the deep-seated gore of an older brother who teased her cruelly at a tender age. They would not feel as she had felt the absence of a smart career path, successful love affairs, rugged wilderness vacations or the reward of a walk-in closet crammed with chic clothes. They would fail to see the visceral grief of a husband not snagged, the white wedding that never took place with its sentimental walk down the aisle on the arm of a father now long dead, the children not born, the roads not taken, the song not sung. They would not hear the sad, blubbering soundtrack to every major holiday, the words of reproach from slimmer, more prosperous relatives. They would not experience the peculiar solitude of unrealized dreams.

Sickened, the neighbors and first responders would wade through the lone woman's vitals and approach what remained of the bathtub. There, they would draw back a scrap of linen curtain and find propped on the rim a seeping, lonesome head with a surprised look on its face.

But why surprised? Had she not imagined this, foreseen it? Was this not the penalty for fat? Not death, that was not the penalty, not being cut to pieces while she bathed. But fear. She knew that her roomy claw-foot tub was made of cast iron and not likely to crack open like a walnut shell. And yet somehow she forgot this as she approached her bath each night.

This was the price to be paid for obesity, climbing into her tub with the distracted look of an aristocrat jouncing in a tumbrel on its way to the guillotine: needless fear. The drainage of deep shame.

1
Never Never Never Land

WHO IS HE, REALLY? Is he young? No. Old. How could death be young? Will he be intimate? Will I feel his eyes boring into my soul, probing for the vanishing point where eternity begins? Or will I be indifferently dispatched, one among billions, someone he does not know or wish to know, ever.

Perhaps death is what he appears to be, nothing, all the nothings he leaves behind: the stilled pulse, emptied stare, silenced voice. Or maybe he is everything, everything a frightened child could imagine, a juggernaut with a thousand faces created from indigestible bits of shock and awe.

When I was young, he had the large, half-human eyes of King Kong. I was 4 when my older brother made me watch the original movie on TV. I have a dim memory of my brother sitting on my chest to keep me in the room. My safe world vanished when that great ape's eyes popped suddenly on the screen, dumb eyes, wild eyes, peering through a high-rise window, indecently curious and covetous of the tiny woman within.

The random actions of the beast-in-the-city horrified me. There you are, riding home on a commuter train from a hectic day at work, skimming the evening paper, wondering what's for dinner, and suddenly, without warning or one word of explanation, for no reason other than the fact that you boarded at precisely the wrong time, a huge, leathery hand reaches down, picks up your train and hurls you into the abyss. Everyone screaming. Or singing. Which is what they did in *Titanic,* another movie I should not have seen, not then, not when I was desperate to think the world a safe and happy place.

After *Titanic,* the world became the deck of a sinking ship with its passengers trapped, horrifically aware of their mortality. They have run out of options, they are going down. A father has spurned his 10-year-old son, having learned the night before that the boy is not his biological child. But when the boy gives up his seat in Lifeboat Number 6 to make room for a woman, the father proudly announces that he is indeed his son and that he feels as tall as a mountain standing beside him. Reunited, they go down together, singing "Nearer, My God, To Thee."

Is he the intruding eyes of the beast? Or the ache of souls waiting to be swallowed by the sea? They could see it coming, those noble gents, they would die aware, singing to a God that may or may not be.

Is he at least decent? Or is he as callous as the doctor whose nurse had called in sick that day, the pediatrician who told my mother that she could leave if she had things to do—so she said fine, I'll go shopping and she left me alone with him—undressed. Is he as smooth, shameless, and narcissistic as the deviant who turned a routine physical exam into a buried memory and a child's bare body into a toy?

"Mommy? What happens to people when they die?"

I asked because a friend of the family had just "died" and was being spoken of in subdued tones. I was 5. I knew about King Kong and the Titanic and I knew I did not like doctors. I did not, however, understand the mechanics of death, such as where people went when the dying was done.

After some thought, my mother replied, "When people die, they go away and they never come back."

I remember waiting for more. There had to be more. We were snapping green beans I had just picked from the garden, dropping the tips into a small paper bag with the edge rolled down and tossing the beans into a dented aluminum colander. I waited for more, but apparently my mother had finished.

To make sure, I asked, "They never come back?"

"No. Never."

Again I waited. It was a golden summer evening in the country. My mother and I were engaged in the mid-twentieth-century rite of waiting for father to get home from work, with brother playing war in his room, making machine-gun noises inside his cheeks, sister quietly fussing in a playpen nearby, tapping a ring of oversized plastic keys between the wooden bars, green beans pinging when they hit the metal colander, and from outside, chickens clucking pensively in the coop, birdsong turning lazy with the approach of night and farm machinery grinding in the distance.

I asked again. "They go away and they never come back?"

"Never."

"Never, never, never?"

"No. Never."

That was it. End of discussion.

I never had trouble sleeping before my mother told me the truth about death. And it was the truth. People do go away and tend not to come back. But the truth overwhelmed me. Suddenly, horribly, death was the nothing that came from nothing, a falling out of the universe into emptiness, out of time into forever. Not even forever. The void.

There were nights when I woke suddenly, my brain stuck inside a sensation of traveling through nothing forever. But *not* forever, because forever assumes that time exists. I could not tolerate the cosmic ride for long. If I did not pull back, sit up and turn on the light, if I kept on hurtling through eternity, where space-time and self had vanished, I was sure I would go mad. As it was, I ended up in a silent tantrum, pounding my fists into the pillow in protest because this going-on-forever-that-wasn't-even-forever was the worst thing I could think of. It was death and death was being Nothing without end. No, not even Nothing. Just nothing.

Sometimes I forced myself to stay awake late into the night. *Some*body had to be watching in case the house caught fire.

Is he the menace that made me wary when I should have been asleep?

Is he the incessant wail of emergency sirens in the city? Having been moved from farmland in Western New York to a dead end street on Staten Island, at night I took to piling pillows over my head in an effort to block out the shrill reminder that somebody somewhere was always in trouble, sick or hurt, and terrified.

The banshee wail of sirens? Or those uneasy feelings stirred up at the 50-cent Saturday matinee, my horror when the astronaut's tether to the ship disconnected and sent him floating off into space—into nothing forever—with a paralyzed look on his face or my revulsion when the scientist fed blood to the severed arm of the Thing From Another World in an effort to keep it alive.

Now I was 8. Had he—the fear of him—become the compulsion to steal? And to overeat?

"Tell the world. Tell this to everyone, wherever they are," said the reporter at the end of *The Thing from Another World*. "Watch the skies everywhere. Keep looking. Keep watching the skies."

Which is precisely what we were doing. One Sunday afternoon, the city's air raid sirens went off and stayed on longer than they should have, far too long for a test. After about 20 minutes, fathers started coming out of their houses to scan the skies. Mass death would come from above. My grandfather was building a bomb shelter in his backyard. The number of Duck and Cover drills at school seemed to be increasing. People looked queasy at the mention of another world war.

I should have known better, but one day I said to my mother, "I don't understand. What's the big deal? Grandpa went to WWI *and* WWII and he came back. Daddy went to WWII and *he* came back. Why is everybody so worried about World War Three?"

My mother looked thoughtful and dismal and answered, "Because that will be the war that ends the world. *Nobody* will be coming back from that one."

On the subject of death, it had not occurred to her to follow up with the odds of heaven or reincarnation. On this occasion, she neglected to mention the United Nations. Or the hope of treaties or détente. It did not occur to me to ask. What I did was look tearfully at my youngest brother (there were five of us by now) and cry, "But Matthew is so little!"

Death was bad enough. The death of *me* was worse. But nothing could be badder than the molten destruction of every living thing on the planet and the forgetting of all history, the reduction of man to a state of being as though he had never been. The strain of the Cuban Missile Crisis, when we came eyeball to eyeball with the other fellow and thought the unthinkable thought of all-out nuclear war, remains with me to this day.

I remember dressing for school one October morning in 1962, probably not aware that our military forces had gone to DEFCON 2 (defense readiness condition), but aware enough to feel alarmed by my mother's absence from our morning routine. I found her in the driveway tossing blankets, canned goods, and jugs of water into the back of the station wagon.

"Mom, what are you doing?"

"Getting ready, just in case."

"Getting ready for what?"

"World War Three. Marty? If you hear sirens, get your coat, find your brother and sister and go outside to the front of the school. I'll have Paul and Matt with me, so just wait, and we'll come pick you up."

"But where are we going?"

"We'll drive up to the Catskill Mountains, we should be safe there."

We had moved again, from Staten Island to Tuxedo Park, which was 40 miles north of Manhattan. My father worked in Manhattan.

"But what about Dad?" I asked.

"Oh no, we won't be able to wait for him."

"Why not?"

"He's in New York, that's the first place they'll hit."

Death again, of my body, of the world and all the souls that ever lived. Was there hope, were there peacekeepers on the planet, was there God? And Dad—how could we just *leave* him? How could we be safe without him? And how were we going to escape nuclear annihilation by driving to the Catskills?

Is death the wasting loneliness I felt 20 years later when my mother called and mentioned in passing that my sister had tried to kill herself again? I burst into tears. My mother scolded, "Oh for heaven's sake, Martha, this has been going on since 1971, you should be used to it by now."

What happens to people when they die?

They go away and they never come back.

I never got used to the fear of losing my brilliant, prophetic, super-sensitive sister. I never knew when she was going to spin out of control, or if she did, what the consequences would be, hysterical laughter or rage, both of which could be terrifying, but even so, my worst fear remained losing her forever.

I never conformed to the prospect of death—any death—my sister's, my own, my cat's, death in general, the stark-raving idea of death, the absolute wrongness of it, the cruel joke of it, the waste and mortal wound of it. Throughout my teenage years, the only nightmares I remember concerned the ending of the world. It ended in one of three ways: nuclear war, alien invasion or the collision of planets.

When people ask, "Why get so worked up over something you can't control?" I want to scream, "But that is precisely the point!"

Perhaps death is the cold steel that years later pierced all my defenses when the doctor in the emergency room at Brattleboro Memorial Hospital held up a graph that had just come back from the lab.

"Do you see this line?" He pointed. "This line right here?" I could have sworn he was smirking. "This line indicates that you've had a heart attack."

I stared for a moment at some empty, infinite space between the results of my blood test and the plans I had made for that day. "That's ridiculous," I said. "I feel fine. I want to go home."

But they did not send me home. I lay confined to a gurney by the embarrassingly inadequate coverage of a hospital gown, tethered to a heart monitor and caught in a tangle of oxygen tubing, sticky electrodes, an IV, and a blood pressure cuff that clamped my arm like a boa constrictor at regular intervals. They had brought my heart rate down with a traumatizing injection of adenosine, and except for the shock of the drug, which had lasted a matter of seconds, I really did feel fine.

I had come to the ER to be told that I was having an anxiety attack, that's all. *A heart attack?* Impossible. I felt torn between two responses: calling everyone stupid-ass fools, ripping off the IV tubing, electrodes and wires, leaping up and storming out of the ER to get on with my day; or collapsing into somebody's arms and screaming, "Oh my God, am I *dying?*" I was trying to decide if the doctor really was smirking or if he just had a perpetually pleased-with-himself expression.

There was some talk about sending me upstairs for the night. For observation. I replied, "Oh no. No no no no *no.*" I hated hospitals. I had managed to avoid them for 54 years, except for the last 4 hours of my father's life, which had not made me any fonder of them. I never got sick. I almost never went to the doctor. As for drugs, even aspirin disconcerted me.

Somehow, and for reasons not fully explained, it was decided that I should go to Dartmouth-Hitchcock Medical Center, the shiny, state-of-the-art hospital outside Hanover, New Hampshire, an hour away. They were turning me over to the experts. I got pretty quiet after that. I asked how I was going to get there. They said in an ambulance. I asked them to call my priest. The handsome nurse named David, who had been watching over me since my arrival at the ER, offered to ride up with me. It seemed uncommonly kind.

But really, this was nonsense. I was healthy. I ate nutritious, unprocessed food. I worked out. I never got sick. I had no idea what it meant to have a fever, cold or flu. But the doctors at Brattleboro Memorial Hospital had looked at my 54 years and 324 pounds, my untreated diabetes, and my smoking habit, and thrown me into an ambulance and sent me off to the specialized care of Dartmouth-Hitchcock's genius physicians.

Weeks later, a friend who is a nurse told me that sometimes

when doctors find a patient who can be still be "saved," they make a point of putting the fear of God into him or her. If that was the game plan behind my abduction, to scare me into making critical lifestyle changes even at the risk of raising a demon or two, I would have to say they overdid it. They had no idea what they were unleashing.

I sat in the back of the Rescue truck on that cold, sunny January afternoon, still hooked up to an IV and a heart monitor, with a blanket draped over my shoulders, making small talk with the uncommonly kind David and an EMT named Hannah, who happened to be the young daughter of my primary care physician. I kept the conversation going, as though obligated to keep them entertained, while alternating between feeling super real and wildly unreal. This stood so far beyond my routine and the scope of my life experience that my ability to grasp what was happening flickered unreliably like the flutter of white sunlight at the truck's dusty back window.

At one point, I asked, "Am I in trouble?"

David said, "No, I don't think so." His tone was warm, gentle and reassuring. "I think this is your wake-up call."

I had been kidnapped. Well-meaning people who did not understand my immense capacity for fear had whisked me away to a lonely place where cigarettes were not an option. All I had with me was my purse. I did not even have my glasses or the cleaning solution for my contact lenses, no comb, no toothbrush or floss, lipstick, ChapStick® or Tums, no music machine, nothing to write on, nothing to read. I did not own a cell phone, I had no way of contacting anyone, I had no family nearby. (I am told my priest arrived at the ER 3 minutes after we left.)

I was traveling in the wrong direction, north, miles away from my friends, my belongings, my books, and my home, all that was familiar and consoling to me.

They go away and they never come back.

2
Who's Calling Please?

HISTORY OF PRESENTATION

Fifty-four year old female diabetic presents to Brattleboro Memorial Hospital on day of admission with chest pain. States that she woke up this morning with severe "indigestion" and a pressure sensation radiating into her chest, neck and left arm. She describes that it was painful at one point. No associated symptoms—sob, diaphoresis.

This lasted one hour and then dissipated and was taken over by severe anxiety, which she describes as an adrenaline rush. She was then very jittery and sweaty all morning but continued to reassure herself. Later in the afternoon she went to the emergency department.

W HEN PRESENTED with patients in need of acute care, the 62-bed hospital in Brattleboro often defers to the mammoth Dartmouth-Hitchcock Medical Center an hour north in Lebanon, New Hampshire. With its academic affiliation and research facilities, Dartmouth-Hitchcock is, in the words of its web site, internationally renowned, nationally ranked and regionally respected. In the words of my ER doctor, "We just want them to check you out." (Read: "If those guys can't scare you half to death, nobody can.")

While I felt secure about being passed off to internationally re-nowned cardiologists, I could not help wondering what made my case so urgent as to warrant their attention. Upon arrival, David and Hannah wheeled me to the Cardiology Section, where, again according to the website, 25 full-time board-certified academic cardiologists specializing in all aspects of cardiovascular disease awaited to provide state-of-the-art comprehensive services, expand the frontiers of knowledge, and train the next generation of academic cardiologists, all of which might have impressed me had I not been harboring a lifelong aversion to doctors.

David and Hannah assured me I was in good hands, which at that moment seemed less important than the fact that my friends from the ER in Brattleboro, my last links to home, were wishing me well and leaving me in the hands of strangers.

Over the next 5 days, while riding an explosive emotional surf and weathering a deluge of worst-case scenarios, my initial misgivings about being left with strangers found support in a collective deficit of problem solving skills and attention to detail.

The first thing I asked for was a telephone. I got one, along with some garbled explanation as to why I could receive incoming calls but not make outgoing ones.

"I don't understand. I have to let people know where I am."

I kept waiting for someone to offer me the use of his or her cell phone or to enlighten me as to what other patients did so I could at least call my mother in Pittsburgh. This seemed of little or no concern to the providers of "high-quality, patient-focused care" popping in and out of my room.

I asked for a disinfecting solution so I could clean and store my contact lenses overnight. Oh no, I was told, we don't have anything like that here. I asked for a toothbrush. I'll see what I can do. Not until the next day did I get one, along with toothpaste, soap and a comb. Was there a bookstore nearby where I could buy a book or a magazine? Yes, there was a nice big store down on the first floor, but I was hooked up to a heart monitor and I wouldn't be allowed to leave the ward. Oh. Well then. Could somebody go to the store and pick up a Times for me or maybe a good mystery? No, there's nobody here who could do that. What about a book trolley, do you have a book trolley on this floor? A what? By the way, I haven't eaten since breakfast. Can I get some dinner? We'll see. Five hours later, at 11:30 P.M., somebody brought me a packet of saltine crackers and 4 ounces of apple juice.

I spent the evening fighting off hunger pangs and panic, cursing myself for not bringing a husband along, for not having a husband, someone, anyone, to look out for my interests, and all the while craving—with heart, body, and soul—a cigarette.

In the whole time I was at Dartmouth-Hitchcock, no one acknowledged the fact that after consuming two packs of cigarettes a day for the past 40 years, I had just inadvertently quit. Cold turkey. They seemed puzzled and a little put out by my weeping fits and electrified state of anxiety, as though nicotine withdrawal was something that everyone else endured with icy calm. If I had known there were massage therapists on the staff, I would have asked for a massage *every day*, but nobody told me and nobody thought to counsel, advise, or even sympathize with my unceasing, insane desire for a smoke.

Bug-eyed and raggedy-haired, scantily dressed in an undersized johnny, hog-tied to an IV and a heart monitor, looking soulfully into the eyes of everyone who entered the room for assurance that I was not on the brink of death, I began to feel like the mad first wife in the tower.

> HOSPITAL COURSE #1
> *She was admitted to DHMC ICCU. Labs were sent and her Aggrastat™ and heparin™ gtts were continued. Aspirin, beta blocker, and statin were started. Her biomarkers were positive but EKG remained without signs of ischemia. Cardiac echo completed and showed no wall motion abnormalities.*

As to the state of my health, I remained in the dark. Except for the pounding on my nervous system, I felt well. In fact, I was getting a needed rest. I had been assigned a large single room. I was being waited on by a platoon of smiling people and having spirited conversations with a number of them about their jobs and their lives or asking impertinent questions about what they were giving me or doing to me and why. I was waking up at 6 in the morning to watch reruns of the original *Star Trek* series while awaiting breakfast in bed and, after my best friend lent me her phone card, to spend much of the day chatting on the phone.

Still, I had no clear idea as to why I was there. It had been decided that I should undergo a cardiac catheterization, but not until Monday. I had arrived Friday afternoon and the geniuses had weekends off. Over the next 4 days, four different people, three of them doctors and one a nurse, came into my room and offered four different reasons for my incarceration.

Number 1: I was fine, really, this was just a wake-up call. (Oh good. No—wait. She's humoring me, because it's one o'clock in the morning and they haven't been authorized yet to give me Xanax.)

Number 2: pssst, by the way, your enzymes are going down fast, which means that it probably wasn't a heart attack, after all. (Phew! But—wait. What does *she* know, she's a *nurse.*)

Number 3: of course it was a heart attack; yes, it could happen again at any time; yes, this is potentially very dangerous, but we won't know for certain until we get a look inside. I would say that we definitely need to do the catheterization. Risks? Oh yes. Well—some. I called him Dr. Death. There was something about him that made me want to be a smart-ass. "I'm from Brattleboro. We don't go to doctors when we're sick, we don't go to the *hospital*. We go to naturopaths and Reiki masters and past life regressionists."

Dr. Death issued a faint, tart smile to indicate that he had dealt with loonies from Brattleboro before.

Number 4: yours is not a problem for the plumbers, but for the electricians (said the electrophysiologist). The real issue here is the SVT, which means that your heart beats rapidly for a reason other than exercise, stress, or fever. Usually the episodes are caused by faulty electrical connections in the heart. Something misfires. Why? Well, we're not sure. Why now? Age, perhaps, but don't worry, it's not life threatening and we can fix it. (Thanks, but no thanks.)

It worried me that in the 5 days I inhabited that dank and dusty room, no one from housekeeping came to clean it. The bathroom smelled moldy and a little bit off and the floor over by the bay window with the breathtaking view of a snowy landscape looked gritty and dirty.

The same absentmindedness attended the circumstances surrounding my departure. Monday afternoon, after the cardiac catheterization, I was told that I would be able to go home on Wednesday. So I contacted a friend and arranged for a ride back to Brattleboro. For Wednesday.

Tuesday morning, I was having breakfast, wondering if I would have to give up coffee as well as cigarettes and concluding that if all coffee tasted like what I was drinking at the moment, it would be no great sacrifice, when a nurse walked in, looked astounded and blurted, "What are *you* doing here?"

"I'm here until tomorrow morning," I answered, looking almost as astounded as she.

"Oh no you're not! We need you to be out of here by this afternoon!"

When friends arrived that evening to take me home, the removal of the IV needle from my hand was so hastily and clumsily done that blood spurted everywhere, spattering my face, my purse, and my clothes. The supervising nurse wished me well and sent me off without a wheelchair. I hobbled, having been bed-ridden for 5 days, what felt like miles down to Dartmouth-Hitchcock's internationally renowned, nationally ranked, and regionally respected front doors.

I could not get out of there fast enough. And yet the minute I got outside, when I encountered the first blast of cold air on my blood-spattered cheeks, I felt sick with fear.

For 5 days I had engaged in almost continuous conversation, with family and friends on the telephone, and with an endless procession of hospital staff, who arrived either smiling or looking pensive and preoccupied, to measure and monitor me, feed me, educate, medicate, advise, and console me. Now I was on my own.

I was on my own and dimly aware that my old way of being had been challenged, that something inside me had shattered. During my stay at Dartmouth-Hitchcock I had felt awkward and alien. For me, hospitals were foreign, even hostile, territory. Big pharma was corrupt. Male doctors were genuinely creepy.

Amid the commotion, variations of the same question had persisted: who am I? Who is this person lying here in the hospital? Not *me*. This isn't the sort of thing I do, so who is *she*? Do I know her? Why don't I recognize her?

Occasionally I found myself stepping outside and viewing my body from above as if I had died, risen up, and stalled at the ceiling for one last look. Institutional environments tend to highlight bodily flaws and what I saw down there was not pretty.

There she was (not *me*), a middle-aged, big-breasted, big-bellied woman, sprawled over a hospital bed, sans make-up, sans clothing, sans peace of mind. She was pathetic and solitary and fast approaching some gray, purgatorial phase just beyond midlife without any of life's prescribed assets or achievements. She was the consequence of all her decisions, and considering her present circumstance, the model of a person who had made all the wrong choices in life.

.

PRIMARY DIAGNOSIS

1. ACS-NSTEMI
   (Acute coronary syndrome – non-ST elevation myocardial infarction)

2. SVT
   (Supraventricular tachycardia)

Secondary Diagnosis

Diabetes, not on meds
Hypertension—untreated
Hyperlipidemia —diet-controlled
Anxiety—has seen a therapist for past 10 years
Lower back pain
Obesity
GERD
Tobacco use

I managed to reach my mother my first night in the hospital by charging our 10-minute call to my home phone number, which showed up on my bill a month later as a $98 transaction.

My mother sounded frightened. She did not ask many questions, but rather, made tsking noises and doomful sighs throughout our curiously brief conversation. I knew she was thinking it, but she had the good sense to omit any remarks about my weight finally catching up with me. She had never been an ounce overweight in her life.

After we hung up, I felt more scared and alone than nurtured. My mother was a spry and healthy old woman. But she was, after all, 83 and she greeted my news of a "possible heart attack" with a timidity I was not accustomed to hearing in her. She sounded frail and elderly. I had scared her. Now she was scaring me.

I had half-expected and half-hoped that she would jump into her car and drive to Vermont to take care of things, the way she had done 17 years earlier when my brother Paul spent most of the summer in the psych ward at Dartmouth-Hitchcock following one of his periodic nervous collapses. An associate professor of music at Dartmouth, Paul had plunged into a clinical depression that required, among other things, electroconvulsive therapy. Over that summer, my mother drove from Pittsburgh to Hanover and back again five times to help shore him back up and provide relief to his wife.

After speaking with my mother, however, after hearing the tremor in her voice, that little-girl-lost tone of voice, I knew that her ability to be *present* was forever gone. My father was gone, too, literally, the iron-willed, dutiful Dad who had driven from Buffalo to Vermont through one of the worst snowstorms on record to fetch Paul home following one of his earlier periodic nervous collapses. Although nobody in my family had ever leapt into a car, plane, or train to rescue me, I felt orphaned sitting in the hospital that evening, rather desolate to think that the parental option was no longer there.

The rest of my family was scarcely heard from. I got one call each from Joe, my wealthy big brother in Washington, D.C. (but not from his wife or two children); Paul, now a Pulitzer Prize–winning composer living in Manhattan; his wife, an editor with her own imprint at a major publishing house, calling from a book fair on the West Coast; my beloved Aunt Martha in Maryland; and my beloved nephew, a junior at Northeastern University in Boston, and the only one of the lot who sounded upset.

Except for Aunt Martha, they were never heard from again. No flowers, no cards, no offers to come to New England and help me "settle in" after my release from the hospital.

My bipolar youngest brother Matt was out of reach, living and working in Oman. My bipolar sister, who couldn't call because she didn't have long-distance service, sent me one of the most thoughtful and loving cards I had ever received. I knew she would have come to caretake me if absolutely needed, but she was living in Western New York with her own agoraphobic tendencies and, if truth be told, I did not need a person in the house who was potentially more unbalanced than I.

My first visitor from Brattleboro was a woman I hardly knew, Anne Shepard, a lovely woman with a doctoral degree in thanatology. The study of death and dying. Perfect.

The nonprofit organization I worked for had just sponsored Anne's most recent training program, a 2-day workshop for health practitioners based on a bereavement model she had created.

While coordinating and marketing the event, I had come to appreciate her graceful air of sanity and serenity.

Just on the underside of 60, soft-spoken, always stylishly dressed, a gentle and thoughtful soul, Anne said that she couldn't really explain why she had come to see me. She hardly knew me. But something had told her upon awakening that morning that it was the right thing to do.

She presented me with a mandala coloring book. She also gave me a pint-sized teddy bear and a sparkly crown made of gold and purple stars that had been used as props in the bereavement training. She said she didn't know why she had brought the items she did, particularly the gold and purple crown, but something had told her it was right.

I still have them. Even the starry crown. I cherish them because of what they represent.

This is not a story about starry crowns or pint-sized teddy bears. It is a story about helpers and healers, people who bring relief and little tokens to a relative stranger because they recognize that that person is on a journey and has reached her point of no return.

Which brings us to Michele. Best friend. She is the one who went to my apartment and found everything on my list: books to read, notebooks to write in, and special fountain pens, my glasses, contact lens cleaner and toiletries, my shoulder bag with makeup and other amenities, and my teddy bear, called Bear.

Staunch and understanding, Bear sat at my side all day in the hospital and slept with my arm curled around him at night. I am grateful for the fact that no one made me feel like the lunatic I must have resembled. ("What's his name? Oh. Just Bear?") He had been my mother's and she had given him to me at a time in my life when I had needed extra nurturing. He's a bristly sort of bear, stiff-limbed and not silky, but his bright, unchanging expression conveys unchanging love.

Michele was the one who lent me her phone card so I could start calling people. Michele was the one who drove up the next day and stayed until visiting hours were done. And when I got home from the hospital, she was sitting in my living room watching TV. She had let herself in, turned on the heat and the lights and waited so that someone would be there when I arrived. Even though she had to rise early for work the next day, she did not leave until the Xanax kicked in and I felt reasonably ready to be left on my own.

I stayed up awhile longer that first night home, unpacking the pads of paper, notebooks and pens I had asked Michele to bring to the hospital. I was grumpily aware that I had not touched them during my stay. I was incapable of imagining, however, that I would not be writing anything coherent in my diary for the next three and a half years. Writing was how I made sense of things.

At the hospital I failed to write or even read. Instead, I talked to friends on the phone, I talked to the people streaming in and out of my room, I stared out the window at the bleak midwinter landscape for signs of a benevolent world, stared at the TV for hints of normalcy, and stared at the ceiling for the automatic writing of angels eager to answer my questions about who this new person could be, would be, was.

I had been kicked out of my comfort zone and there was no going back to it. I knew this from Day One at the hospital. I knew it the moment I encountered the hum and buzz and institutional hues of life in Room 503, when the reality of where I was—and why—finally occurred to me and I knew, I knew on some hateful, subliminal level that after 40 years of inhaling two packs a day, I would never smoke again.

HOSPITAL COURSE #2
She was scheduled for cardiac catheterization.

A visit from Dr. Death overshadowed Sunday, Day 3, at the hospital. He was a trim, shorthaired, rather natty man with a smug air that set my teeth on edge. I believe I have already mentioned that male doctors unnerve me, which contributed in no small part to the hair-raising quality of my experience at Dartmouth-

Hitchcock. It was a major medical center and a teaching hospital and the bastards were everywhere.

Dr. Death headed my team, and the time had come for him to discuss my case. I had had a heart attack, he said. Is it bad? It could be, we don't know the extent of the damage. We can't really know until we get a look inside. Am I in trouble, is this something that could kill me? Most certainly, and possibly within the next 3 months, which is when second heart attacks usually occur.

I understand that most people on the planet would react badly to these words, but I also think there is a special circle of hell-on-earth reserved for people like myself who suffer from an overactive imagination, a panic disorder, a death anxiety, and a highly contentious relationship with God—when I am willing to say there is a God—or an acute case of existential nausea when I am not.

Dr. Death sat in his chair with his head tilted back, either to rest it against the wall or to reinforce his superior air, while I sat in a helpless heap on the bed watching my life flash before my eyes. I don't recall the details of our conversation but I do know that while being argumentative, my clever brain in its clever way was also fishing for a dozen different kinds of reassurance that I still had a good long healthy life ahead of me. Dr. Death would not, could not, offer that reassurance.

I also got consent forms to sign. For cardiac catheterization. Risks? Yes, there are risks. While complications are rare, they can be deadly. Like—oh, I don't know—heart attack or stroke, should the catheter tip dislodge a blood clot from the inside wall of the artery. Or blockage of blood flow to the arm or leg below the area where the catheter was inserted. (Surgery may be required to restore blood circulation.) Abnormal heart rhythms. Kidney failure (caused by the contrast material). Pericarditis (infection or inflammation of the membrane lining the heart). Pneumothorax (an accumulation of air in the pleural cavity). Or my favorite: puncture of the heart or one of its blood vessels, which may require immediate open-heart surgery to repair.

Dr. Death left me in a demented state of suspense, in which I overlooked the more likely complications (pain, swelling, tenderness, bruising at the catheter insertion site) for hallucinations of doom while waiting to be served what could have been my last meal on earth. After dinner, when I asked the attending nurse for reassurance—but I'm all right, really, I'm still healthy, my heart is good?—she answered in a weary way: there are no guarantees in life. They don't really know. They won't know until they get a look inside. You've made your choices. How long have you been smoking? And you look like you could lose a hundred pounds.

She whisked off to attend to other patients or to take a break from all our want and need. I began to feel abandoned. It was 8:30. There were no more people flitting in and out of my room. It was getting quiet out in the hall. I was alone. No cigarettes. *And no chocolate.* Nothing good on TV. I tried reading, but my mental juices had frozen. The words on the page fogged up and floated away.

I started calling people. I called my mother, Aunt Martha, Michele, friends Phyllis and Kate. For the first time ever, I called my priest and my therapist at their homes.

Everyone sounded gentle and caring. But no one could tell me I was not going to die. I didn't even ask. How could they have known? They had heard the words "heart attack" and were probably more frightened than I was. (No, wait. That's not possible.)

My fear that evening had nothing to do with anxiety. My fear that evening was actual fear, real fear, which imparted an air of unreality to the night. Again, I experienced an eerie disconnect between me and *her.*

She was a miserable creature. When I looked at her, she turned away. *She* turned away because she had failed. She had no husband, no children and at the time no significant other. She lived alone in a musty second-floor apartment with water stains on the walls so spectacular they once moved a Comcast technician who was also an abstract artist to a state of rapture. ("Look in the bedroom," I said as he raced about in pursuit of ever more interesting patterns. "There's one that looks like Africa!")

She had no house; no property; no second income; no stocks, bonds, or savings; a job but not a career; and no retirement plan, no IRA or pension, nothing, *nothing,* but a fairly pleasant existence in

Vermont and a childhood dream that would not quit. She had $120 in her checking account and $25 dollars in her savings account and the only other thing she owned was a 17-year-old Toyota Corolla. She didn't even have the spinster's consolation of cats. Her two substitute children cats had died a year before, and she was still too grief-stricken to think that they could be replaced or to risk experiencing that much pain again.

A lifetime yawned between where I was at the moment and where I had meant to go. There were dreams still in the making. I had never been bored in my life, not for a second, and there remained a century of things to do. Death was not an option. And yet both the doctor and the nurse had stressed only uncertainty. Maybe yes. Maybe no. We won't know until we get a look inside.

I was terrified of what they might find when they looked into my heart.

On the phone that night, my Episcopal priest, a gay, 20-something man with a powerful faith and presence, focused on regrets. Is there anyone in your life you want to make amends with? Is there any one you want to forgive or whose forgiveness you seek? (No, not really.) My therapist, a former Methodist minister, focused on one of our many topics: the importance of knowing that although life is uncertain, although I am not always in control, I can handle whatever happens. I am okay, even in death.

I did not believe this, of course, which was why I was still in therapy, and I relied on Xanax and mental exhaustion to get me to sleep that night, a night that I will always associate with Nietzsche's words, "And when you gaze long into an abyss, the abyss gazes also into you."

If I died, who would care, really, and what was I leaving behind?

Hospital Course #3
The cardiac catheterization was completed including the placement of a stent to her RCA

Day Four. I woke up early the next morning, weeping. I wept all the way to the cath lab.

The worst thing about the cardiac catheterization is that while they make an incision in your groin, pass the cardiac catheter into your blood vessel, advance the tube through the blood vessel up into your body, inject dye through the catheter into your heart, move the catheter tip into various positions inside the chambers or vessels, and watch everything on the imaging screen, *you're awake!* Then, if deemed necessary, which it was in my case, they perform percutaneous coronary intervention. This means inflating a little balloon inside your artery to improve blood flow and then inserting a small expandable wire tube called a stent to hold it open and *you're awake!* The sedative drugs they give you may be powerful but I could still feel the wires poking around inside my heart and I could hear the evil doctors talking: This looks fine. This looks good. Nice. Oh—no, wait a minute, what's that? Uh-oh.

Fortunately it did not take more than an hour. And when it was over, Dr. Death appeared out of nowhere all smiley-faced to say that everything looked good, the damage had been minimal and I was fine. He kept smiling and he put his hand on my shoulder, and suddenly I wanted to sit up and hug him to pieces.

"I'm okay?"

"You are okay."

And I went back to weeping some more.

HOSPITAL COURSE #4
The patient remained anxious and tearful throughout her stay prompting a Psychiatry consultation. The results of the consult was that the patient will follow with previous therapist. Other recommendations included an SSRI and implementation of cognitive behavioral therapy. Patient declined additional medication at this time and stated she would pursue CBT with her therapist. Electrophysiology consult called to evaluate patients SVT. It was determined that no ablation was necessary. The patient declined further medical treatment for her diabetes.

On Day 5, during my final meeting with Dr. Death, I asked, "Tell me once and for all. Did I or did I not have a heart attack?"

It was quite some time before he spoke. He was leaning back again in his chair against the wall to give that arrogant upward tilt to his chin and I had returned to feeling combative. Finally, he said, "You've had the smallest of heart attacks."

"If this hadn't happened just now, would I have just gone on and found myself in real trouble a few years down the road?"

"Possibly."

"May I consider this my wake-up call?"

"You may."

It was up to me to decide who had called and why and how I would respond.

And while Dr. Death talked about making lifestyle changes and taking advantage of the excellent Cardiac Rehabilitation Program at Brattleboro Memorial Hospital, I had the most peculiar and wonderful sensation. I sensed the presence of angels. Not very many, maybe one or two. They seemed to be situated several feet above the doctor's head.

I'm not here to argue about whether angels exist or not. Just trust me for now: they were there. Small and loving, yellow, sun-lit faces suffused all around with a brilliant, almost blinding gold. They were talking to me through this man. Telling me things I needed to know.

Something about dying first before I could live again.

3
An Unbearable Sequence of Sheer Happenings

I GOT HOME FROM THE HOSPITAL on a Tuesday night. I was expected back at work the following Monday. It did not seem fair or fitting that I should get only a week off for a heart attack, but not much happened at the office unless I was there, primarily because at that point I was the only one there to do it.

As usual, when blessed with multiple consecutive days off from work, I expected to write. I had been maintaining a diary since age 11 and the first thing I anticipated doing was to give a full account of what had just happened to me.

I did not. I could not. Writing required silence and solitude. The magnitude of my fear made it impossible for me to sit home alone in a sustained state of abstract, self-examining thought. It might have been denial. If I wasn't telling my diary about it, maybe, just maybe, it wasn't happening.

Also required for any kind of writing were a pack of cigarettes on the desk, a vintage ashtray, a lighter, a cigarette holder, a thin whorl of smoke and the mysterious power of nicotine to keep the mind focused.

My first day out of the hospital, I woke up feeling both shaken and shaky. I decided against making coffee. I had no intention of giving up coffee but on that first day at least, I thought it best to spare my nerves. It felt weird and disorienting to forgo my morning routine but in addition to sparing my nerves, it reduced the chances of lighting up.

Everything felt weird and disorienting. I had been bedridden for 5 days. I could not imagine summoning the strength to drive downtown to the Hotel Pharmacy to fill the million prescriptions I'd been given.

The doctors had prescribed what is known locally as the Dartmouth cocktail, the standard therapy for first-time cardio patients: a beta blocker, a statin, a blood thinner, and aspirin. Also nitroglycerin, which nobody thought I would need, and Nexium[R] to minimize my chances of mistaking heartburn for a coronary. I was already taking synthroid for an underactive thyroid and Xanax, as needed. I knew that filling these prescriptions was the first order of business, but even a short drive to town felt taxing.

My landlord had a plumbing and heating business next door, where his mother managed the office. I tottered down the stairs and across the driveway and asked Julie for a ride to the drugstore. She not only drove me, but she came inside with me. She must have sensed that I needed someone to lean on, literally.

The pharmacists and staff at the Hotel Pharmacy, where I had been a customer for 30 years, were exceptionally friendly folks—patient, good-humored and compassionate—but as I stood there waiting to be given the terrible, horrible drugs, I felt like an alien in their midst. They were all healthy. I no longer was.

While Julie bantered with everyone up on the dais, where the dirty business of filling bottles with pills took place, I stood like a crestfallen child too embarrassed to participate. I had failed to keep myself in good health.

I had not honored the promise I had made to myself 30 years before when, while visiting my grandmother and rummaging through her kitchen for cereal, I opened a cabinet door and found the entire bottom shelf taken up by prescription drugs. Translucent orange, red or yellow, crisscrossed with green and blue labels, the little plastic bottles glowed in my mind like a store of radioactive material.

Cautiously I tried reading their inscrutable labels and imagining my grandmother's world. I wondered what it felt like to be elderly and sick enough to depend on a bumper stash of pills, beginning each day with a measured intake of tablets and capsules, including drugs to treat the side effects of other drugs, and then winding down at night with still more pills to calm the digestion, the heart, the nerves. I swore to myself then and there that I would never have a cabinet full of drugs. At her age, I would not need them because I had lived healthy and true.

At that time in my life I was showing a strong preference for alternative therapies. In addition to a monthly massage, I scheduled frequent visits to the chiropractor and the acupuncturist. Although I had no exercise routine, I did not have a car and so I walked everywhere. I took tonic Chinese herbs, I had stopped drinking alcohol to excess, and I ate whole grains, plenty of vegetables, and a minimum of processed foods. Except for my annual visits to Planned Parenthood, I sought traditional medical treatment so infrequently that one year my doctor's office called to ask how I was doing and suggest that I make an appointment just for the hell of it. (I didn't.)

Whole grains and deep tissue massage. They alone would keep me fit to a ripe, fully functional old age.

Drugs were evil, drugs were bad. Any drug. Back in high school, I had been surrounded by every recreational drug conceivable and available at the time, and I had traveled with the pack that used them daily, but I had abstained. I don't know why. Drugs were everywhere. People served them on silver platters at parties. They dropped them into thermos bottles at lunch. Afternoon classes dissolved into chaos because half the students in the room were tripping their brains out.

Although I remained within easy reach of recreational drugs throughout college and beyond, I never touched them, not even pot. Drugs were toxic. They were foreign invaders. All drugs, even Xanax. It had taken my doctor 4 months to convince me to start synthroid and 2 years to talk me into Hormone Replacement Therapy for early menopause, which I quit 5 years later when the Women's Health Initiative discovered new risks. I routinely tore up prescriptions for antibiotics, and I had been successful in dodging the lithium, anticonvulsants, antipsychotics, and antidepressants foisted upon my younger siblings at various hair-raising and heart-breaking times over the years.

Pharmaceuticals carried the taint of financial deals between Big Pharma and consultants who advised the FDA and determined the efficacy, usage, and market value of drugs. They were the devil spawn of corporations implicated in the suppression of unfavorable research results, manipulation and fraud, disease-mongering, and off-label marketing.

Drugs were, above all, dangerous. The prescription bottles that I carried back home with me that first day out of the hospital might just as well have been concussion grenades. Or coiled vipers. I brought them home anyway. That's how scared I was.

The pharmacist had included a two-page printout for each drug. I did not have the nerve to read them, not yet. *How to use this medicine. Important safety information. Possible side effects. If overdose is suspected.* Had I possessed the knowledge to detect possible side effects, I would have catastrophized every tremor, bruise, muscle spasm, hiccough, or abrupt ringing in my ears into a life-threatening development. I folded the printouts neatly and filed them away. It would be three and a half months—after the drugs had proven themselves by assimilating into my body without undue incident—until they felt "safe" enough for me to read.

I had been an anxious person and an alarmist to begin with. I came home from the hospital terrified. I was terrified of dropping dead from a second heart attack. I was terrified that the stents had been improperly inserted and would suddenly, without warning, turn into killer clots. I was terrified that the new drugs would cause hemorrhaging, asphyxiation or anaphylactic shock, if not immediately, then months later. Every morning for the next 4 years I woke up feeling doomed, wondering if this would be the day my heart or stents or drugs failed me.

Imagined death was always at my side. Fear ruled. The joy had gone out of my life.

Joy, cigarettes, and yes, coffee. Deep, rich, bitter, bracing coffee served black in oversized mugs. It turned out that I couldn't go back. Even decaf seemed more than my raving nerves could bear, but the primary reason for abstaining was my inability to dissociate that steaming cup of self-content from a soothing, contemplative smoke.

I knew that from now on the timeline of my life would be divided between BHA (Before Heart Attack) and AHA (After Heart Attack). Before cigarettes-and-coffee and after. I knew that the heart attack, however mild, had just accelerated a tolerable midlife crisis into a war between where I appeared to be going in life and the quite different place I wanted to be. My wake-up call involved a miracle of personal transformation.

The call would be answered. Somewhere, deep inside of me, there lived a wholesome child, a warrior princess and a wise old woman who had put their heads together and proclaimed it possible for an agoraphobic, diabetic, nicotine addicted, 324-pound compulsive overeater, with a panic disorder and dreams deferred to transfigure herself into a mentally whole, physically healthy, professionally satisfied, spiritually fulfilled human being.

A week after returning to work, I had lunch with Anne Shepard, the thanatologist, bereavement counselor and, incidentally, apprentice practitioner of a popular personal transformation program, who had brought me that starry crown in the hospital. Over a virtuous salad (not my usual burger and fries), I confidently announced that, yes, I *had* been thrown for a loop, but *my* journey would take 2 or 3 months at most and that by spring, I would be a whole new person, a reinvented self. Perhaps 50 pounds lighter. Or even 60!

Anne replied in her gentle, pleasant way that it probably wouldn't be by spring, that, if truth be known, I was in for a long, hard ride.

I did not believe her. I had just quit tobacco. I could do anything.

I started smoking when I was 15 years old, back when almost everybody smoked, shortly after the Surgeon General's Advisory Committee confirmed a causal relationship between smoking and lung cancer. The committee's 400-page report claimed that not only was an average smoker nine to 10 times more likely to die of lung cancer than the average nonsmoker (and a heavy smoker 20 times more likely), he was also courting chronic bronchitis, emphysema and coronary artery disease.

Apparently the report was front-page news when it came out in 1964. But I was not listening. I started using tobacco in 1968 while a sophomore in high school. We were living in Princeton, New Jersey at the time, a hectic time when the climate at northeast ivy-league schools began to shift from entrenched, conservative elitism to left-leaning activism.

Rebellion, revolution, crackled in the air. While visions of clashes with helmeted cops danced in our heads, we artists and hippies at Princeton High helped our comrades at the university organize demonstrations against war, class oppression, and the draft, Dow Chemical (makers of napalm) and the presence on the university campus of the Institute for Defense Analysis and the Army Reserve Officer's Training Corps (ROTC). Inspired by reports of nationwide marches and sit-ins, we could be found sunning ourselves in open fields cultivating serene cosmic thoughts or skulking in dingy rathskellers strewn with Zig Zag cigarette papers and acid album covers, adding artwork and glitter to banners advocating civil rights, free love and feminism, dividing our time between saving the world and expanding our view of it with recreational drugs.

Although speed, cocaine, and heroin were readily available, the drugs of choice at Princeton High were marijuana and LSD. Dazzled by the mix of politics, drugs, sex, and intense psychedelic stimuli, we were caught up, if not in sweeping historical events, then at least in our own elated sense of history. The United Nations had declared 1968 to be the International Year of Human Rights. Same-day broadcasts from the other side of the world and the awesome quiet of the first moon shots gave new meaning and poignancy to the freshly coined phrase "global village." We were part of something huge, a seismic shift in human consciousness. Cigarettes were a footnote to the Age of Aquarius.

A combination of crusade and chemical activity made us invulnerable. A fusion of affluence, arrogance, and stoned and trippy, hormonal highs fueled the fictive immortality of youth. Nothing, nicotine least of all, could touch us.

I recall smoking in school. There is a black-and-white photograph of me seated in the front row of the school auditorium during a rehearsal for *The Show-Off* costumed in 1920s dress, with a cigarette in my hand, taken moments after I had emitted a cloud of smoke so dense it obscures the faces of the people slouched beside me. Back then everybody smoked everywhere.

Well, not everybody. My parents did not smoke. They had quit to discourage their children from starting. Come to think of it, I don't remember anyone using cigarettes in my extended family on either side. My Croatian, Italian, and Greek uncles brought out cigars on special occasions, like convening in the living room to watch football after Thanksgiving dinner, and my Grandpa Howe smoked a pipe so habitually that the smell of cherry tobacco still conjures him up for me.

I am told my great-aunt Eleanor smoked, but she lived in Birmingham and we never saw her.

My two younger brothers, ages 11 and 8, did not approve of my habit. Apparently they had read the Surgeon General's report. One frosty autumn evening they sneaked into my room, snatched up my pack of Marlboros and dashed away, alternating between nervous twitters and triumphant guffaws while I followed, screaming murder. A mad and merry chase through the house ended in front of a roaring fire, where my brothers giddily tossed my cigarette pack into the flames.

I was furious, humiliated, and completely unconvinced. I went out and bought another pack. The Surgeon General, while proclaiming its peril to one's health, had underestimated the addictive properties of nicotine. Quote: "The tobacco habit should be characterized as an habituation rather than an addiction."

It never occurred to me that I was hooked. I *liked* smoking. In the 40 years that I smoked, I gave little thought to quitting. I never once tried. I might still be smoking now if I hadn't spent 5 days in the cardiology section at Dartmouth-Hitchcock. My wake-up call urged me to attempt something I never promised I would do and never thought I could do. And never even wished to do.

Occasionally I would strike a bargain. I remember pledging to quit when a pack went up to a dollar. Or I would quit when I turned 40. Or I would taper down to "social smoking," a sad misnomer considering the fact that by the time I made this particular bargain, smokers had been relegated to the status of medieval lepers, who were formally and publicly declared dead to the world.

In college, while I was stage managing and doing props for a production of *The Threepenny Opera*, the director asked me to go out and purchase cigarette holders for the prostitutes. It was not difficult finding cigarette holders in those days. Tobacco shops, wonderful, wood-paneled places with pipes and racks of newspapers and things that smelled like *men,* could still be found on Main Street and in malls, along with a head shop or two.

When I showed up at rehearsal with a bag full of plastic cigarette holders, I joined the actresses as they practiced waving them about. I loved it, and after that, never smoked without one. I got to the point where I could not tolerate the rough, round feel of a cigarette, even a filtered one, on my lips. The cigarette felt intrusive, leafy, and dirty; the holder felt clean, sleek, and prophylactic.

It might have been a form of denial. I could tell myself I wasn't smoking, not really, because the foul weed was at a safe remove, although there was no denying the evidence of what I was taking into my body when frequent cleanings with pipe cleaners drew out gobs of sticky black tar.

At any rate, it was distinctive and slightly eccentric to smoke with a cigarette holder, and I was always searching out new ones, collecting different lengths, colors, and styles. I hated the ejectors and I would never have bought a holder with rhinestones. I scoured antique stores for holders made of ivory, ox bone or amber, tortoiseshell, Bakelite or jade, holders intricately carved or trimmed with gold and kept in small, silk-lined, leather cases. It was all very vintage and flapperesque, and it became my signature, part of my style, an affectation for which I was known and admired. Cigarettes and their paraphernalia had grown integral to my image, even my self-identity, and worse, vital to my functionality as a writer.

When I came home from Dartmouth-Hitchcock, I lived for a week with an unopened carton of Viceroy Lights stashed in a drawer of my desk. They were there, there for the taking, and my body was in shock for the want of them, but I did not touch them. That's how scared I was. Scared of dying.

After a week, my therapist asked what they were still doing there; why hadn't I thrown them out? I responded with a blank stare, unable to answer. The thought was unspeakable. A house without cigarettes was like a body without a core. My therapist replied in the flat, grim tone he uses when he tires of my enormous capacity for denial: I wasn't serious about quitting as long as that carton remained in my desk.

The next day, I asked Michele to come over and remove the unopened carton from my house. As she took it from the drawer, she asked, are you sure about this? I nodded, speechless.

Heartsick, I followed her to the door and in that moment when she crossed the threshold between the inside and outside of my home with my cigarettes in a plastic grocery bag, I experienced a sudden fell swoop of panic, a steep pang in the pit of my stomach and a plummeting sense of abandonment. My best friend (and I don't mean Michele) was walking out the door. Cigarettes had been my helpmeet and mainstay for most of my life, just an arm's length away, as intimate as a kiss, as steadying as a hug, almost as cozy as a warm body in bed, as present and committed as a mate.

Since it was equally vital for me to lose 120 pounds, we had also rounded up my chocolate stashes in the house and added them to the plastic bag. The dark chocolate covered almonds, the Nutella, the frozen mini Snickers bars.

I made another bargain. I told myself I could start smoking again on my seventy-fifth birthday. Or eightieth, perhaps, if I wanted to live to be 100. And I do.

As for my Great-aunt Eleanor, the one who lived in Birmingham, she chain-smoked all her life. I am told she was the defiant kind of smoker, the kind who, when asked to refrain from lighting up, lit up and blew smoke in your face. I am also told that when she turned 90 years old, she developed a slight cough.

And quit.

Insomnia, fatigue. Nausea, cramps. Constipation, gas. Tingling in the hands and feet. These are known symptoms of nicotine withdrawal. Sore throat, dry mouth, foul tastes, bleeding gums, postnasal drip. Headaches. Tightness in the chest. Sweating, jitters and shaking.

Not everyone experiences every physical symptom. The only ones that I could claim were mild versions of chest tightness, jitters and shaking.

Anxiety. Depression. Despair, confusion. Inability to concentrate. Now this sounds more familiar. Cravings, yearnings. Loneliness. Nighttime awakenings. Yes.

Increased appetite and weight gain. Not good. Irritability, anger, rage. Temper tantrums, intense needs. Also not good.

These were the symptoms I feared most: Weight gain. And rage.

I had always heard that people in withdrawal could turn mean or at the very least, irritable. I had not planned my smoking cessation. I had not rearranged my lifestyle, my relationships, hormones, or brain receptors in advance of the trauma of quitting. I just quit. It was pretty simple: I did not want to die. Ever. I quit and I stayed quit without a support group, nicotine patch or gum, lozenges, inhaler or spray. Fear of death was my nicotine replacement therapy.

I had plunged headlong into "the system," the vortex of florescent-lit hospital visits, kindly technicians and harried doctors, rides in Rescue trucks, booklets, brochures and print-outs with instructions, scary tests and procedures, prescription drugs, bewildering bills, and one-sided arguments with automated health insurance drones.

The words, "You've had a heart attack" had laid bare the truth that I was addicted to a substance closely related to cocaine, morphine, and strychnine. I had finally absorbed the fact that as a smoker I was sucking in the same carcinogens, toxic metals, and poisons used in producing plastics, batteries, pesticides, rat poison, cleaning fluids, and fertilizer and the same chemicals involved in preserving dead bodies, creating car exhaust, and taking life in Nazi death chambers.

The two symptoms I feared most did not occur. I did not gain weight. I joined Weight Watchers, stepped up my exercise routine and lost 20 pounds in the first 3 months.

My other fear, that a lifetime of rage would surface, dissolved in tears. I did not get mad, I cried. While my body set about the business of flushing out 40 years of tar buildup, my psyche released a lifetime of grief.

Unexpected symptoms showed up in what I lost. I lost my voice, literally, as well as my story. A week after I quit tobacco, I began to notice that my voice had turned raspy. It faded, sometimes failed altogether after 2 or 3 minutes of continuous use. At work, people on the phone either complained that my cell was breaking up or wished me well with my cold.

All my life people had described my speaking voice as musical and my singing voice as lovely. Two weeks after quitting cigarettes, when I opened my mouth to sing in church, I discovered that in addition to being hoarse and husky, my voice would not stay in place. I had no tone and no ability to sustain a melodic line.

I could not sing. I could not write.

It was impossible to write without a cigarette in my hand and impossible to organize my hospital experience even into diary entries. I may have seen angels twinkling over Dr. Death's head, but as long as I felt deprived of voice and a story, life became what philosopher Hannah Arendt said it would be without the meaning story reveals: an unbearable sequence of sheer happenings.

Somehow I had to turn the unbearable sequence back into a story. But without my writing, I would have to process my experience in new, as yet unknown ways.

4
Nighttime Awakenings

I COULD NOT SING, I could not write. So I wept. I have always been a weeper. I can sob over a dead chipmunk. I can burst into tears just watching an ant nudge his dead or wounded comrade across the floor.

As a child, I was scolded for my outbursts more often than consoled.

When I was 12, while watching one of those Walt Disney nature docudramas in which a folksy narrator pretends to know what wild animals are experiencing and thinking, I choked up because something died. A mother or a mate, a cougar or coyote. Or maybe an otter. Who knows? I left the room in hysterics. My mother followed me around the house yelling, "Stop this! Get a hold of yourself! If you're going to carry on like this, we can't let you watch these things!"

One day when I was 20, I remember sitting on the living room floor listening to music and breaking down over a failed romance. My mother looked up from her newspaper and called from across the room, "Are you crying? Stop it, stop it right now. Is this about that James person? He's not worth it, you're disgracing yourself, stop!"

When I was 37, six months after my father died I called my mother on the phone and said tearfully, "Mom? I miss Dad." I believe she actually sputtered and stammered for 30 seconds before answering. "Oh? Oh—but that was 6 months ago. You should be over that by now."

My mother never succeeded in making a man of me. Despite her efforts to convince me that emotions were useless because they were not rational, I remained a weeper. The weeping, the hair-trigger sniffles and crying jags, multiplied and magnified with age. Two years after my father died, I went into early menopause. Tears flowed more freely than ever. When I returned to the Episcopal church after a 30-year absence, I sat in the last pew for the whole first year and wept uncontrollably with the torrential energy of flash flooding. Then when I quit smoking: deluge. I skipped over a lifetime of rage and went straight for the grief.

Although research continues to explore the function of tears and to seek an evolutionary context for them, it is believed that for the majority of human beings weeping is a good thing. A big old sloppy cry can resolve grief, alert us to the fact that something is wrong, signal to others that we need help, stimulate the production of endorphins and prove salubrious to our hearts, stress levels, and overall health.

Tears that do not exit the body can rankle into anger, bitterness, or weakened immune systems. I believe the results would be illuminating if we could measure the number of diseases, divorces, and clinical depressions attributable to unshed tears.

Two weeks after my heart attack, I sat in the stress lab at Brattleboro Memorial Hospital weeping. There I was again, back in disgrace, back in a hostile environment, waiting to take a cardiac stress test, wearing a too-small Johnny and feeling like a beached whale while a male technician stuck electrode patches to my shameful body. In our polite small talk, we never acknowledged the fact that I was awash in tears.

And neither did the cardiologist. He was new in town. I knew nothing about him and he knew nothing about me, nor did he wish to apparently. I do not recall that he even looked at me. He entered the room, nodded in my direction, picked up my record from Dartmouth-Hitchcock and after scanning its content, said, "Oh, this is completely manageable."

I should have felt relieved but I did not. I should have taken his words to mean that my case was not a serious one. And yet I went on weeping, perhaps because his pronouncement had not developed into a conversation about my feelings or concerns. I cried through the whole stress test, and afterward, when I told the doctor that I had given up smoking and would be going to my first Weight Watchers meeting that week, he bustled his way to the door, muttering, "Yes, well, that's all well and good, but we'll see if you're still doing these things a year from now."

My eyes pinned desperately on him and delivered a fresh load of tears as I asked, "So then, you think I'll still *be* here a year from now?"

"Well of course!" he barked while the door swung shut behind him and he strutted off to his busy, important life as Brattleboro's brash new cardiologist.

While I dressed to go home, any remaining tears were probably due to the realization that my injured parts—my shattered psyche, shattered confidence, shattered equilibrium—rested in the hands of this cocky, dismissive, barking man.

I would be happy to report that anxiety and panic disorders had been invented to legitimize people with weak minds and a predilection for hysterics. I would love to say that the trick to "curing" an anxiety attack or a phobia is to just buck up. But the social stigma is simply not the case.

Considering the fact that I had two bipolar siblings, a third with a history of periodic clinical depression, and a fourth with a huge thirst for alcohol, in addition to a bipolar second cousin and a bipolar grandfather, whose mother was severely agoraphobic (and those are the ones I know about), I considered myself fortunate to have gotten off with a panic disorder.

But with it came a profound fear that I, too, would one day succumb to the "family curse." In her desperation to avoid blame for bad parenting, my mother insisted on attributing her children's emotional breakdowns and psychotic episodes to an inherited chemical imbalance, which reduced my experience of depressed or delusional siblings to a nagging apprehension that it would be a mere matter of time before I also snapped or became immobilized and nonfunctional and tagged for the psych ward.

Panic disorder has no single recognized cause or one sure cure. I don't know that it ever will. It may always be considered an unhappy mix of genetic, biological, and environmental factors with different therapies for different people. What I do know is that my wake-up call had alerted me to the fact that I was never going to be any crazier than I was at that moment, that I had been crazy long enough, and that it was time to take care of this—this *thing*.

Whether due to imbalanced neurotransmitters or childhood trauma, my whole life had been a cycle of fearful daytime and nighttime awakenings fueled by a sustained sense of disquiet and dread. Suddenly I was well into middle age and still afraid. It was now or never. So I wept. I released trickles, I released torrents of nicotine-soaked tears in hopes of dispelling not only the toxic biological byproducts from my body but also the crazies from my soul.

Anxiety, in one form or another and to varying degrees, had traveled with me my whole life. In addition to fearing, loathing, and despising death from an early age and struggling at night against a sensation of falling without end into the void, I became a habitual liar at school and eventually a kleptomaniac. At home I fretted about deadly snakes in the cellar and sometimes in the evening I put off sleeping as long as I could because *somebody* had to stay awake all night in case *something* happened.

When we moved to the city, I lost sleep not only over the incessant wail of sirens, but over worst case scenarios as well, one of which involved my mother getting off the subway and the doors whooshing shut right behind her, leaving me helpless and alone and hurtling through sinister underground tunnels to points unknown.

I told her I did not trust those subways. Sadly, it did not prevent her from doing things like leaving me alone in front of a movie theatre in midtown Manhattan while she went shopping. On that occasion I just stood there and cried until one of the ushers, who sounded as disgusted with my mother for leaving me there as he was with me for crying, helped me buy a ticket and walked me in.

I often felt abandoned. I never felt safe. What with air raid sirens, air raid drills, the explosive sonic booms of pilots breaking the sound barrier, the Soviet premier Khruschev promising to bury us, I worried incessantly about nuclear attack. The atomic bomb was very dangerous, we were told. It could knock you down. It could throw you against a tree or a wall. It could break windows or burn you worse than sunburn. It could end the world.

I was too young to smoke, so I ate.

At age 12, although we had moved from the city to the affluent community of Tuxedo Park, where no siren sounded ever, I was still waking up in the middle of the night racked with terror. On those nights when my metaphysical pangs felt like living death, I would get up and walk down the hall to my parents' room to drag my mother out of bed and ask her the impossible questions. Why are we here? What's the *meaning* of it all? What's the point of *living* if all we do in the end is *die*?

I don't recall her answers. I only remember the anguish and despair that brought me to her.

When it occurred to me one day that at school we had stopped doing the duck-and-cover drills, I asked my sixth grade teacher why not. She replied that crawling under a desk or throwing yourself to the ground and tenting a newspaper over your head were no longer considered adequate protection against nuclear attack. Soon we would be asking: will the living envy the dead?

The kleptomania stopped after a store clerk caught me slipping booklets of stickers into the hood of my coat. When my mother arrived to pick me up and found me sitting with a cop, I made a deal with her. If she promised to never tell my father, I would never steal or lie again. (I kept this promise.)

The stealing stopped but I still had to eat, didn't I?

Onward to Princeton, to high school, where I lost weight and came out of myself long enough to consider acting as a career, something I was being encouraged to do by our drama teacher, a conscientious man who normally made a point of steering his graduating students *away* from the long odds of show business.

After high school, we moved again, to Buffalo, into a large, comfortable house with wide windows and a wraparound porch overlooking Lake Erie. I buried myself. I had decided I would rather be a novelist than an actress, and having decided that novelists could educate themselves, I shunned college and took advantage of free room and board with my parents.

I lived in a room in the attic with exposed timber and beams, with neither flooring nor insulation, and wrote novels and began to go mad. Although my room bore an agreeable resemblance to a bohemian garret, the fact that it was unfinished was cannily symbolic of the fact that I should not have been there.

I should have been distinguishing myself at a great university or blazing my path in the world, and I did spend summers or parts of summers in Aspen, Colorado; Chautauqua, New York; Lenox, Massachusetts; and Jackson, New Jersey; but I always returned to the Gothic house set on the edge of a 60-foot drop into Lake Erie.

The house was not literally Gothic; it just felt that way. Some of our neighbors on Lakeshore Drive had given names to their homes, balmy names like Lakehaven, Windy Acre, or Whispering Oak. My siblings and I christened our property Rapidly Eroding Cliffs, a droll reference, conscious or not, to the psychological problems that were closing in on all of us, with the exception of our mother, whose Master's degree in psychiatric social work seemed to have made her wise in the ways of professional distance (or healthy denial), and our big brother Joe, who was finishing up at Harvard.

We lived a good distance from the city, but I worried about our safety, increasingly so as my father came home most nights in an anxious, nervous state and ranted at the dinner table about what a corrupt and dishonorable, amoral and unprincipled, dark and dangerous place the world had become.

Our wraparound porch had a number of glass-paned doors with flimsy latches. The knob to the back door to the house, which led to the laundry room, felt alarmingly loose. I mentioned to my father one day that we might want better security for the house. He answered that there would be no point in it.

"Marty?" he said. "If somebody is determined to break into

your house, it doesn't matter what you do. They will find a way."

I became a nocturnal creature. After routinely checking the locks on all the doors downstairs, I climbed upstairs to my cold garret, put on a pair of fingerless wool gloves, and stayed up until dawn, drinking coffee or cocoa laced with peppermint schnapps, chain smoking, writing, keeping watch. I had breakfast with my parents and siblings and after everyone had left for work or for school, I went to bed and eventually fell asleep despite my pestering fears that something terrible would happen to one of my family out there in the big bad dangerous world. I usually had supper waiting for them when they got home.

It was inevitable that I should stop leaving the house altogether. I began to think of cars as fiery death traps. (I had not yet learned how to drive. In the same way that I had refrained from drugs in high school, I had never considered getting my driver's license. Don't ask me why.)

Night and day I watched members of my family come and go and worried about their safety until I laid eyes on them again. Day by day the world outside became more and more treacherous. Occasionally I walked a mile down Lakeshore Drive to pick up a carton of cigarettes and probably some Twinkies or Ring Dings at the corner store, but even that stopped when I found my father was willing to pick up my cigarettes. Sometimes I went with my family into the city to attend an exhibit at the Albright-Knox Art Gallery or a concert at Kleinhans Music Hall, but my phobia about cars finally took over. For 4 months I did not step foot outside the house.

And during that time, the house itself became dangerous. I developed a fixation on the furnace in the cellar. I decided that at any moment, it could blow, blow big, blow us all to kingdom come. The possibility remained real in my mind, ever present and terrifying. One evening, while walking through the kitchen, I decided that the dishwasher sounded rough and I started to worry about that, too. For weeks I worked myself into fidgets wondering which would blow first, the dishwasher or the furnace.

On one particularly devil-ridden night, at two o'clock in the morning, while gazing outside my garret window I noticed a string of white lights floating over the lake, moving evenly and slowly toward Buffalo's busy harbor in the distance. A UFO. It had to be. What else? The aliens had finally arrived to obliterate our world. I became so distressed that I considered calling the cops or the FBI or maybe even NASA, but after 2½ hours of sheer agony trying to decide whether the lights were *on* the lake or hovering just above it, I got the bright idea of looking up the shipping news in the *Buffalo Courier-Express* to see if a ship was scheduled to come in at that hour. It was. I made some buttered toast and went to bed.

I grew hypersensitive to grisly items in the news. I remember becoming truly distraught over a mutilated woman who had been found without her arms in a bathtub and failing to see the humor as my friends spent the evening working references to *Arms and the Man* and *A Farewell to Arms* into the conversation. Another time, after reading about a policeman who had been cut nearly in half when a suspect's car slammed him up against the hood of his cruiser, I kept envisioning the scene. I imagined over and over again the moment when the cop saw the car coming and realized what was about to happen. These things haunted and hurt me and defined the world. Nothing good. All bad.

Shortly after the Night of the UFO That Turned Out to Be Cargo Transport, it occurred to me that I might need professional help. I knew that my parents had been taking my sister to a psychiatrist in the city, so one night I pulled my mother aside and said, "Mom? I think I might need help. I've been acting a little crazy and I think I may need to see somebody about it."

My mother sighed heavily and answered, "Oh no, Martha, not you, I can't bear it. You're the strong one. You're the healthy one."

My father was disintegrating before our eyes, so disappointed was he in the way the world was turning out and in the downward trajectory of his once-brilliant career in public relations for the once-mighty Bethlehem Steel, which he could see was sinking fast. My brilliant sister, who was creating brilliant oil paintings, drawings, and etchings at this time, made her first suicide attempt. My brother Paul wept openly and often because he wanted to be a classical composer but my father wanted him to apply his brilliant

48

athletic ability to a brilliant career in baseball. My youngest brother Matt, who wanted to be a brilliant rock star, was falling apart along with our father, who accused rock musicians, and anybody who wanted to become one, of being in league with the Devil.

I don't know whether my mother did me a disservice or a large favor by denying me my neuroses. I do know that shortly after our conversation I realized I had a choice to make between leaving home and losing my mind. I applied and got into Syracuse University as a theatre major.

I was assigned to a spanking new, swank and shiny, high-rise dorm glaringly, almost obscenely, located on the edge of a low-income section of the city. City? During the application and interview process, it never occurred to me that if I got into Syracuse, I would be living in a city. I did not like cities. Too many sirens. Too many strangers. Too much random crime.

To make matters worse, due to an administrative oversight, I did not have an assigned room, so they threw a bed and a desk into a "typewriter closet" and installed me therein, far away from the snack machines, fully applianced suites, and girlie-girl fun that was supposed to make college a hoot.

I felt so claustrophobic and isolated, and so threatened by the street crime right outside our doors, that I got myself transferred to a hippie style co-op in a rambling Victorian house on the other side of town. Any hopes of feeling safer, however, were dashed by the disappearance of a co-ed freshman last seen hitching home for the weekend. And by the events at Munich, when Palestinians kidnapped and killed 11 Israeli Olympic athletes.

There were mornings when I would set off for a class on the fourth floor of a building, get as far as the third floor, use the bathroom, glance at my frazzled self in the mirror, and then turn around and walk back to my room, insanely alert to the risk of encountering enraged Black Panthers before I reached my front door or Arab terrorists or serial killers who preyed on co-ed freshmen witless enough to hitchhike alone. Despite the anxiety attacks, avoidance behavior, and stress, I managed to get straight A's that year at Syracuse, but I had no intention of going back for more.

Since my mother wasn't going to find me a psychiatrist and since I didn't know a soul in Buffalo, I concluded that the best way for me to manage my fears was to find a place in the world where I could feel safe.

The first Broadway musical I ever saw was Bob Merrill's *Carnival* in 1961 and my favorite song from it was, not the more popular *Love Makes the World Go Round*, but *Mira*. In this very sweet ballad the heroine wistfully tells her new friend in the city about Mira, her hometown beyond the bridges of St. Claire where everybody knew her name.

I remember staging and singing this song over and over. At age 21, I must have remembered it as an expression of something I valued. So far, I had lived on a chicken farm in the country, a dead-end street in the city, a gated, mansion-studded enclave, a suburban, ivy-league community, summer cabins in the Catskills and islands off the coast of Maine and most recently Rapidly Eroding Cliffs overlooking Lake Erie, but I had never lived on Main Street. Main Street, as built, shellacked and utopianized on Hollywood back lots and as exemplified by Beaver, Pennsylvania, the small town that both my parents grew up in and left as soon as they were able. Main Street. The place where everybody knew your name.

I still had scads of family in and around Beaver, but Beaver was situated outside Pittsburgh in southwestern Pennsylvania, too close to West Virginia, which was South, and to Ohio, which was Midwest. Being a born-and-bred East coast snob, I turned my eyes toward New England. A small New England town. Preferably with a college, for the culture.

I chose Middlebury, Vermont, as the cure for my nighttime awakenings and my morning, noon, and evening jitters. Until I could find a job and an apartment, I rented a room in a local woman's house where, ironically, my first night's sleep in Vermont was shattered by the woman's daughter pounding on the front door at two o'clock in the morning with her three young children in tow, seeking refuge from a drunken, abusive husband on the rampage.

A year later I moved to southern Vermont to attend a small liberal arts college with an outstanding theatre program. In Putney, near Brattleboro. After college, when it came time for me to be on my own, apparently the most important thing was to *belong*. Brattleboro seemed a good fit. It struck me as the kind of big small town that just took you in. Whether you were a low-residency psychiatric patient from the Brattleboro Retreat, a Colombian or Japanese student at the School for International Training, a Cambodian refugee, or an aging hippie with an antiquated value system, you were tolerated, you were absorbed.

I wanted roots, a home, where everybody not only knew my name but also understood my soul's command to calm my terrors and weep all of my tears.

So after my heart attack, I wept. I discovered a helpful connection between tears and a reduction of anxiety.

Even so, after 2 years of magnificent weeping, I asked my therapist, "How long is this going to go on? How many tears could I possibly have inside of me?"

He didn't seem to know and I am still one of those people who can't watch a nature show because something invariably gets killed or separated from its mother, and I still cry in church at least once a week, if not 10 times, with or without music, and dear God, don't ever put a baby in my arms.

And yes, I will cry for that tiny ant pushing his wounded comrade across the floor, especially if some unbearably poignant music happens to be playing in the background. I will cry because he is so persistent, loyal and valiant in the face of his reality and I will cry just because life is so goddamned sad. It is sad and there is nothing we can do about it. All we can do is to be vigilant about what we should *not* do. The worst thing we can do is to *not* feel the sadness, to *not* weep, to *not* acknowledge the hurt that sits at the core of the human heart.

5
Imaginary Friends

IT WAS MY THIRD SURPRISE VISIT to the doctor's office in a week's time. By surprise I mean unscheduled, unannounced, and half-crazed. It was still only my first week out of the hospital.

I had already met with my therapist and priest, both of whom came to my home out of respect for my convalescence. Their generous listening skills enabled me to start making sense and a story out of my experience, which I hoped would give it meaning and a new direction, but it was the doctor who could perform the most vital task at this time: administer an EKG and assure me that I was not having a second heart attack.

Dr. Sczesny was a woman, young, vital, and big-hearted, German born and German trained, who rode her bicycle to work and homeschooled her three children. She deliberately underbooked to avoid stress and burnout. She always had time to listen to my concerns.

She still does. She is compassionate and patient about my anxiety attacks, although she openly puzzles over why I don't seek relief in meds. She has a sharp, sometimes goofy, sense of humor and the refreshing ability to say the words, "I don't know." Most importantly, our visits possess the quality I now demand of all my consultations with health practitioners: that I leave their office with a buoyant step, confident that whatever my condition, there is something I can do about it.

Over the years, Dr. Sczesny and I have marveled over the fact that indeed, we *do* not know, we are *not* in control, that perfectly fit people can drop dead at age 45 and that perhaps the healthiest thing we can do is to make our peace with uncertainty. Uncertainty. My foe. And still I leave her office feeling strong. There is more science than God to her and yet there are times when our talks feel plaintively spiritual.

When I think of my first 2 weeks home from the hospital, I hear static and see a blur. I still did not have a clear idea of what had happened to me or what my condition now was. I assumed that my questions would be answered when I met with the cardiologist and started the Cardio-Pulmonary Rehabilitation program at the hospital, but these events were 2 weeks away. In the meantime, my imagination raged.

So I had landed in the doctor's office for the third time in a week, deranged by my phobia about prescription drugs and my apprehensions about keeling over in the middle of the night with no one around to pick me back up, lip quivering, and asking, "My God, how am I going to get through the *weekend?*"

Dr. Sczesny, who had once again taken me in at a moment's notice and had just informed me once again that my EKG looked fine, suggested that I invite my friends into my home, ask them to organize a relay support team with people coming over in shifts until I had adjusted to my new circumstance and grasped the fact that I was not in constant danger.

Dr. Sczesny also said the words that I would hear repeatedly over the next 4 years from doctors, paramedics, therapists, and priests: Martha. Take. The. Xanax.

There were two reasons for my reluctance to pop a tranquilizer every time I began to unravel. First, I felt on the verge of unraveling all the time, which meant I would be popping Xanax all day and all night into day again, which I preferred not to do. And second, if I waited for those special moments when it felt like I was bursting out of my own skin or BASE jumping inside my skull, I feared that if I started dying as well, I would be too serene or uncoordinated to get myself to the ER, crawl to the neighbor's, or call 911 for help.

It was coming home from work to an empty house, it was looking into the empty space of the evening, it was getting through the night; it was waking up alone at 6 and trying not to go into a panic over having a second heart attack because that was the hour when I had had my first. It was looking at an empty weekend when everyone went off and *did* things, but not me because I had built my life around channeling my spare time and mental energy into writing, but suddenly, I could not write and I could not sing and I could not be silent, solitary, and still. Here was another loss: independence. Feeling helpless, quite hopeless on my own.

I had lived alone most of my adult life. It was something I knew how to do and I was proud of the way I had managed to stare down the cultural assumption that a woman who remains single in life is defective. She is an incomplete human. Or an unrealized lesbian. Or something to be pitied and then scorned the moment she starts amassing cats.

Despite bouts of celibacy and severe loneliness, I had come to understand the advantages of living on my own: there were no sacrifices, no compromises, no other person's behavior to rein in or restrict, no one to nag but myself. I answered to no one, I set my own schedule, lived by my rules and made my own life choices. I suffered my own consequences and nobody else's. I could be bold and spontaneous, although I rarely was, but I *could* be. I liked falling asleep with a man at my side and I liked waking up with him; I loved that slow, lazy talk in the cool blue of dawn and still-sleepy sex, but the minute we got up, the minute his feet hit the floor, I wanted him out. I wanted the house to myself.

Not anymore. At least not now. Solitude hurt. It was death, it was dying. I had always been a bit of a hypochondriac, but now with the trauma of a heart attack and the full apparatus of the medical profession to back me up, I became a complete one. Every twinge, every muscle spasm, every skipped heartbeat, every intestinal gurgle or pang, new bruise or mole, or speck of blood on my dental floss, every cold sore, vaginal discharge or rash, every episode of dizziness, headache, or gas pointed to a potentially life threatening illness.

I have no doubt that if someone had been living in the house with me at the time, preferably a heart specialist with the forbearance of a saint or a head doctor with the mindset of Buddha, my erroneous thinking would not have gotten such a grip on my nervous system. There would have been someone to talk me down. When Dr. Sczesny suggested that I start calling my friends, she was prescribing the medicine of fellowship for easing the loneliness, fears, and feelings of powerlessness that come with illness. I thought it was a fine idea.

Although Michele was "on call" day and night, it would have been absurd for me to expect one person, no matter how steadfast and generous, to keep me afloat. I needed a gang. But for the first time in my life, there wasn't one.

This came as a shock. I had always had a gang. The concept had been self-evident from the start. When I was a child, we children seemed to outnumber every other living thing, families came in sixes and sevens (which made the family a small gang in itself). Everyone had older brothers to bully or protect them and baby siblings waddling about in smelly diapers. Halloween night resembled the evacuation of a small city, and at Thanksgiving, the population of our neighborhood could triple overnight from an influx of visiting cousins.

My gang was the kids on the city block, the dead end street across from the Staten Island Zoo and adjacent to the YMCA. We poured out of our houses after dinner to play ball games and freeze tag, Mother-May-I and Simon Says, ran back inside at the first jungle of the ice cream truck and begged our Dads for loose change, fell into a concentrated silence over jimmy cones, orange creamsicles[R], and toasted almond bars in the deepening dusk and then, when the air turned thick with fireflies, took empty jars, punched holes in their lids, and filled them with starry light.

As I entered adolescence, social life revolved around cliques and the glandular tug-of-war over who's in and who's out, but now I lived in a small community and more often than not my gang was the whole class embarked on a field trip. We traveled en masse to Revolutionary War sites, natural wonders like underground caverns and movie adaptations of assigned readings like *Lord of the Flies*. We vacillated between scuffling on the softball field and dolling up for dances, between roughing it in combat action role playing games and beautifying ourselves for makeout parties and the Beatles.

In high school my gang was the hippies, freaks, and artistic set of Princeton High. We hung out at Palmer Square or on the spacious lawns of the university campus, dragging our politics, drugs and acid rock from underground parties to protests, sitting up all night in garish diners or crashing at somebody's "pad" on lumpy, duct-taped couches.

In college, I was one of the theatre crowd, a spirited pack of actors, directors and techies, ever and always building sets and costumes, hanging lights, rehearsing Shakespeare, bedroom farces, and arty studio productions until summer, when our department morphed into a professional repertory company for which we provided the labor and bit parts, pulling all-nighters in the scene shop and driving off at dawn in a cloud of sawdust, paint fumes, and tobacco-and-coffee breath to Howard Johnsons for scrambled eggs and ham.

For my first 20 years of day jobbing, I cooked. And for ganging about, there was no place better than a restaurant: everyone sitting down together before the dinner rush to eat and hash over the melodrama of our lives, everyone bitching and crabbing about obnoxious customers and squabbling with each over orders until closing time, when we all gathered chummily at the bar for an instant party and a roaring drunk.

When you don't have a family of your own, it's your gang that gets you through life. For tea and sympathy all you need is one good friend, but for living you need a gang.

For 10 years I cooked at a popular steakhouse known as the Jolly Butcher, which provided me with benefits like being able to call the kitchen guys to come over and chase the bat out of my house or discovering the extreme joy of tennis one summer when one of the waitresses signed us up for lessons or summoning the husbands with pickup trucks whenever I needed to move or haul something away. We marked milestones in each other's lives, taking up a collection to buy a memorable gift or a meal whenever somebody had a new birth or a new house to celebrate, a significant birthday, graduation or an inclination to pick up and move on.

At that same time, my tae kwon do class made up another gang. We formed small convoys to drive to martial arts tournaments and organized bake sales and car washes to raise money for the tournaments we hosted. One year when my sensei learned that I never bothered with a Christmas tree—who for?—she insisted that I host the dojo Christmas party, which forced me to get one. I felt warm all over when she put out the word that everyone who attended had to bring a shiny new ornament to hang on my tree.

When my career path shifted from cooking to office and program administration, I worked 8 years at the School for International Training, the academic branch of a nonprofit, mission-driven organization with an impressive network of international education, exchange, and development programs in over 60 countries.

The Brattleboro site of The School for International Training (SIT) has a large staff spread across a gorgeously situated campus with a dining hall that resembles a ski resort and a diverse, vivacious community created by the comings and goings of students, faculty, consultants, program participants, and distinguished visitors from around the world. There was an ever-present social life to tap into while working there, an underlying grid of support, a vitalizing, high level of energy, and a sense of participation in other cultures through friendships, fashion shows, cuisine-specific dinners, musical evenings, seminars, thesis presentations, and occasionally strenuous debate. The whole world was in on this one.

So you see, there had always been a gang. But not at this time, not now. Entire casts of friends, acquaintances, and extras had disbanded; I had moved on or they had moved on; we had literally separated or just drifted apart. At the time of my heart attack, after a year and a half of unemployment and mostly solitary writing, I was working at another nonprofit, mission-driven organization with a wide array of services and programs but only two staff: the executive director and me.

So I tried rounding up one of the old gangs, members of the bar crowd from 30 years before who still lived in the area, people I occasionally ran into on the street and occasionally celebrated birthdays with, all women, some younger than me, some older, some married, some not.

I called the elder, the one who was already in her sixties, the one for whom we had all worked as bartenders, waitresses, and cooks at her thriving pub on Main Street. When I asked her to put out the word about my situation and perhaps organize a lineup of gatherings and good times, I should have sensed trouble in her hesitation and slight befuddlement. I did not, however, because I was having a vision of something so natural I assumed that everyone would spontaneously and joyously share it.

I was thinking of community. When the author Dan Buettner set out with a National Geographic team of demographers, anthropologists, and medical researchers to identify where in the world people lived longest, and why, he concluded that even more than the plant-based diets of the numerous centenarians living in what he called the Blue Zones, it was their faith-based communities that kept them vital and engaged past the age of 100.

Longevity in the Blue Zone begins with healthy, moderate eating; regular physical activity; and regular, moderate drinking but it ends with a greater emphasis on values reinforced by prevailing behaviors within the culture: an established means of relieving stress, a sense of purpose in life, a strong sense of belonging, a commitment to putting families first and keeping them close, and the luck or inclination to be living in an environment that makes a healthy lifestyle possible.

Invariably, every city on every list of Best Places to Retire has a *manageable, vibrant,* or *walkable* downtown. The proliferation of niche communities, co-housing options, and village models indicates that those in a position to plan for retirement are not planning to retire in splendid isolation. Nor should they be. Studies reveal that the more friends a woman has, the less likely she is to develop physical ailments or depression as she ages, and indeed, another trend in retirement living options appears to be the readiness of divorced, widowed, or never married women to pool resources and move in with each other.

For me, Dr. Sczesny's suggestion conjured images of housewives in ancient Greece gathering for gossip at the well, medieval maidens singing chansons while weaving at the loom, American frontierswomen congregating under the pretext of a quilting bee, contemporary women "doing" lunch or seeking aid and comfort in online health and wellness communities. They are images of women telling their stories, their very own, private stories, finding the words, speaking the words and experiencing those words as received, witnessed, and understood.

I believe that for humans, the most regrettable of omissions, along with unshed tears and unexamined lives, is untold stories, the things not shared, the lost opportunity to be honest about oneself and tender toward others.

I was thinking of the Amish way. The heart's ease of community. The tribe or the clan. The book club, bowling team, church supper. I was thinking of all the friends and neighbors in situation comedies that have been miraculously accessible since *Fibber McGee and Molly*, people who show up for coffee without calling ahead, neighbors who cut through the backyard and appear unannounced at the patio door, friends who enter through inexplicably unlocked front doors without even knocking.

I imagined my friends dropping by with groceries to help make dinner and settle in for a casual, chatty meal, offering to do the laundry or fix things around the house, spending an evening or two, maybe three or four, watching a movie or just hanging out. I did not need advice, analysis, or problems solved, a pity party or a plan. I just needed voices in the other rooms, people around, people to *be* with, friends to come and sit with me like family. I needed a sense of life going on around me, of life going on, period.

When I think about it now, my request for enforced company seems presumptuous, but at the time I only felt like an idiot and a total loser for having to ask. I was not bothered by the act of asking—when it came to asking, I had no shame—but by the fact that the asking was necessary. Dan Buettner observes that in Sardinia, one of the original Blue Zone sites, when neighbors notice that you haven't shown up for an occasion, they go knock on your door to discover why not. They don't program neighborliness into their lives. They live it.

If I ended up disappointed, I have myself to blame for trying to schedule what should have been spontaneous. The girls did their best. But they just didn't get it. They didn't understand. Or they could not be bothered. Maybe they didn't like me, not as much as I thought they did, or maybe these were friendships that had run their course.

A few of them showed up at my door, but only one at a time, and each one only once. Nobody stayed for dinner. Nobody made an evening of it. There was no flow to the initiative, no generosity and nothing gracious about it. One of them called every three nights for a while to check in with me but she never came over. One did accept my dinner invitation but left as soon as she had eaten. Another took me out for a drive on a tour of sites from her childhood in Northfield, which remained the sole topic of conversation.

In the end, it all felt obligatory, like they could not see the need or understand the hell that I was in. I appreciated the effort, but the half-heartedness of it felt more dismal than if no effort had been made at all. I just started to feel embarrassed. I felt pathetic and began referring to these women as my imaginary friends. After a few weeks, nobody called and I have been in touch with only one of them in the 6 years since.

The disappointment reminded me that if I was going to solve my emotional suffering, change my behaviors, and revise my story, I needed to see and confront in my hoard of fat, a lifetime of unmet needs.

At this time I enjoyed telling a story of one of my mother's annual visits 10 years before, when I noticed that my only surviving, energetic, fiercely independent parent was showing signs of slowing down. Frailty had crept into her brain and bones. Gingerly steps in her gait, odd pauses in her speech, a rasp in her voice presaged the onset of true elderliness and slapped me with evidence that she would not be around forever.

Rather than deal with the raw grief of losing her, I decided that I wanted to experience having a Mom one more time. I wanted to come home from work and find her making dinner. The meal could not be done and waiting. It was vital that when I walked in the door, she be in the midst of making it.

I was feeling nostalgic for the days when I felt cared for and catered to, the days of coming home to a light-footed bustle in the kitchen and the aromas of a meal nearly ready. My brothers and sister would be coming in, happy or troubled, anxious for our father to arrive from work so we could gather at our big round table and share the day's news over dinner.

I explained these nostalgic feelings to my mother one morning over breakfast and asked if she could be discovered making dinner that evening. She laughed because she thought it was silly but she agreed.

All day long I looked forward to getting home from work. As I climbed the stairs to my second floor apartment, I began savoring the moment, my senses straining for the smell of fresh-baked brownies and a buttery, lemon-and-thyme chicken with hearty root vegetables finishing off in the oven. Or the scent of rosemary and garlic melting into the fat of roasted pork, the sight of condensation on the windows created by fresh green veggies steaming on the stove, the sound of pots banging and dishes clattering in the sink, radio playing softly in the background.

Halfway up the stairs, I stopped, unnerved by the silence. And the absence of savory smells. With a feeling of foreboding, I opened the door to an immaculate kitchen, where my fit and trim, vegetarian, nutrition-conscious mother stood at the sink, rinsing a wooden spoon.

When she saw me, she said, "Oh! You're here! All right." She scurried over to the stove, opened the oven door and said, "Here I am, dear, slaving over dinner!"

She put on oven mitts and pulled out a roasting pan with a spaghetti squash in it. I'm not kidding. One. Spaghetti. Squash. While I watched in horror, she mashed the stringy pulp with butter and salt, divided it between two plates garnished with patches of arugula and poured two glasses of red wine.

Dinner.

I guess I have always wanted too much.

According to her, while she had been the best mother ever, I had been an annoyingly needy child. I was always wanting or demanding something. Another story I liked telling at this time was that one day, to my surprise, she confessed that when I was a baby, there was something about my crying that irritated her like nothing else. Nobody else's crying wrung her out in that way, just mine. Frequently, her solution was to put me in the nursery and shut the door.

She says she left me alone for hours, crying, in the dark.

Too young to summon up even imaginary friends.

I don't remember this, of course, or maybe I do on a cellular level. I can *imagine* it. I can imagine that baby's terror.

One day my therapist said, "You have a choice. You can be the little girl who stays stuck in grief because she keeps waiting for someone to come into the room, pick her up, and make everything better. Or you can let the Mother die and become the adult capable of processing her feelings and experiences, taking care of herself, and having faith that she is not alone."

She is not alone because she believes in God.

She believes in God—right?

The brusque cardiologist who conducted my stress test attacked my vulnerability at our first appointment. Because I had ignored his instruction to go back to Dartmouth-Hitchcock and have the ablation done for my SVT tachycardia, he started off by accusing me of being argumentative.

After 20 minutes of pointless argument, he concluded, "I know what you want, you want to be coddled, you want someone to tell you that you have nothing to worry about, that everything will be all right. Well, I won't do that, that's not what I do. Maybe you should just grow up."

At this point, he was actually yelling at me and this portion of our conversation was taking place in his waiting room. There were no other patients around, but his staff was there, hearing, or trying not to hear, everything we said. You could have heard him down the hall.

I felt humiliated and furious and the next day I switched to Brattleboro's other cardiologist, the mild-mannered and beloved Dr. Tupper, but I knew that this guy was right. Dismissive and contemptuous, but right. My hypochondria demanded reassurance without end and my need was a bottomless well, sustained by rabid fears of abandonment.

At Dartmouth-Hitchcock, on the night before my cardiac catheterization, while making my distress calls, I left a message for my priest, Thomas. When he called back an hour later, I asked him for the hundredth time why I couldn't believe in God.

Thomas, who must have just come in from a bibulous evening, answered, "Because you're fucking insane, that's why!"

It was an invitation. Stop looking into your mind. Stop looking into your heart. See now what is in your soul.

TWO

Once upon a time there was a little girl who got lost inside a deep, dark wood.

She had learned to fear this place. In the late afternoons, as she and her friends straggled home for supper, they drew closer to each other through the deepening shades of dusk and spoke of the mysteries in the forest at the edge of their village.

They spoke of it in whispers, their brows puckering, their voices growing hoarse, their words breaking up over what felt like gravel in their throats. This forest harbored wolves, bears, wild boars, and all sorts of bedeviled game. It harbored doubt and the unknown and the shadowy launch of the faceless boatman ferrying souls across the river of death.

Some of the older children said they had ventured into the forest. They claimed that it was much like any other forest but they admitted that they had never gone deep into the heart of it and that they had never passed all the way through it and come out on the other side.

She had not meant to go too far. She did not like feeling perplexed and lost. But even in her world gone mad, she could discern hopeful shapes, bliss bodies in the mist, miracle workers urging her to trust uncertainty, just breathe, and let go.

There was no path except for the one she made and no true course until that sobering moment when she realized she had reached the point where turning back entailed a longer walk than going straight through, and so she went on, deeper into midnight, her journey eased by the light of transformational fires.

6
The Space Within Me

WHEN I TOLD DR. SCZESNY that the Old Gang Initiative had failed, she said, "You need to find new friends."

I hesitated. For a year I doubted my ability to present myself to strangers in a favorable light. But then, when Michele left town for 7 months to train in massage therapy at the Cortiva Institute in Philadelphia, a New Friends Initiative became imperative.

I made some valiant efforts but nothing gelled. A woman who was something of a local legend for her extreme political activism in the sixties ignored my suggestion that we get together for coffee and maintained a hard-boiled silence on the treadmill next to mine at the Cardio Rehab class where we had met. The HIV-positive man whose flamboyant personality promised madcap nights on the town turned out to have more problems, hysteria, and paranoia than I felt I could handle at the time.

Before I could accept her invitation to tea, the elfin woman who gave hand and foot massages at the Farmers Market while counseling emotional healing through animal totems and Native American wisdom died in a car crash on Route 30. My sponsor at Overeaters Anonymous, a devout Catholic with a hauntingly spiritual mien, seemed less available after a diagnosis of stage 4 breast cancer.

A very personable younger man, 20 years younger, who inspired fantasies of culinary vacations in Italy—rooming at farmhouse villas; strolling through sunflower fields and medieval towns, vineyards and olive groves; hunting truffles and peeling lemons for limencello—left the country abruptly to work abroad as a political journalist. A most agreeable friendship with a new hire at the office—a vivacious, adventurous woman who gave parties where every guest turned out to be a pagan, a yoga instructor, or Reiki master, and who actually had us sing "The Age of Aquarius" on one of those days purported to be its official beginning—eventually succumbed to bitter office politics.

My search for new friends fizzled. After her graduation from the Cortiva Institute, Michele returned to Brattleboro, got engaged to her boyfriend of 7 years, but disengaged herself within a year when he failed to follow through on too many of the things that mattered. She took her shattered heart to the Mount Madonna Center in California for the summer-long Yoga, Service, and Community Program. When she came back East, she vowed that she could never return to Brattleboro, where memories lay in wait and her ex-fiancé still lived. She moved to the Berkshires in search of a new career and new life.

It had been 2 years since my heart attack. I still wept for no apparent reason, and I still panicked without reasonable cause.

Julie, my landlord's widowed mother, lived next door in a spacious apartment above the family business. Because I also lived in a second floor apartment, I could look out my kitchen window straight into her living room. Our houses were not close enough for me to see anything more than silhouetted lamps and moving shadows but during the bleak stretch of time that Michele was gone, the only thing I cared about seeing next door was lights on in the evening. And the color-streaked glow of a television being watched. It meant that somebody else was home, somebody else was still up—just in case.

Every night while I did the dishes, I looked into Julie's living room. If the TV was on, I felt a little better. It was sad, a bit like Jay Gatsby gazing across the bay, assigning all hope and quality of life to the green light at the end of Daisy's dock.

If the television was not on, if Julie had gone out for the evening or had already retired for the night, I felt desolate. Who would there be to take me to the emergency room if I started dying or went into rapid heartbeat? Who could I call upon if the only thing that stood between me and head-banging insanity was having another warm body in the room?

I felt utterly defenseless against the dread in my soul, a malaise that I call the four degrees of disconnect.

First, there is the shock of plunging into the stunning, unspeakable nothingness of the void.

Second, there is the existential nausea that strikes when confronted with the vastness of time and space, the insight that strips all living beings of significance and life itself of meaning. The vastness is not quite as horrifying as the void because it still holds the possibility that, while disturbingly far away and in a form we cannot imagine, somewhere, somehow, something else exists.

Third, there is the ache. For me, the ache comes at twilight, which is more a sensation than a time of day and more often than not, a hunger no creature comfort can fill. Night begins to fall. It is the indifferent place of neither here nor there, inert and unlit, the interval for winding down and wondering what's next. It's that lonely, empty feeling in the gut, all famine and yearning, the stuff of nostalgia, heartache, and unrequited love.

And fourth, there is pain. The pain that cannot be purged. It has no tears, it cannot weep. It is the implacable feeling of defeat when someone dear has died, the rawness of things that cannot be repaired or retrieved or lived again. It is the opposite of sunrise, the opposite of belonging, believing, and belief. Any and all cords to the business of being human have been cut.

When I found myself peering into Julie's living room for signs of life every night, I realized as never before that I had been fooling myself for years. As a single woman who lived alone, I thought I had been taking care of myself. And while yes, I had been supporting myself, paying my bills; staying healthy and mentally stable; keeping myself educated, enlightened, and entertained; keeping my cats alive; my home cozy and clean; and my car in good running condition, I now understood the unsoundness of my foundation.

It hadn't been courage that enabled me to come home to an empty house most nights to face the void, the vastness, the ache or the pain. It hadn't been sturdy selfhood or the feat of being fully adult that had kept me functional and for the most part cheerful. It had been tobacco, kitties, books, and old movies, my oversized suppers and evening snacks, my secret cozy world and illusions of grandeur.

For much of my life I had watched my three younger siblings periodically turn so bizarre, delusional or clinically depressed as to require hospitalization. For me, total collapse was never an option, a temptation at times, but not a first choice. It may have been the difference between emotional upheaval and genuine mental illness, but I had learned to perceive and receive my breakdowns as directives to keep on healing and as openings for continued growth.

Psychosis is pure escape. Depression is sleep. Fear, however, is a challenge, a spur. It galls me to say it, but perhaps it is my blessing that anxiety was my curse.

After my heart attack, when I began to understand the depth of my new madness and the work that lay before me, I got busy. I did what I always do first when I feel myself slipping. I started assembling a support team.

Because I had chosen to live in a smallish, Main Street sort of town, and because I had stayed for 30 years, I would love to say that I survived and thrived with the assistance of the mythical people in my neighborhood: the precociously perceptive child with pigtails and a steady supply of pink bubble gum; the elderly widow who dispenses pearls of wisdom with her lemon verbena tea and homemade almond lace cookies; the old geezer whose gruff manner masks a tender heart; the wryly disgruntled handyman, the jolly grocer and butcher in the bloodstained apron who saves fresh scraps for my homely but lovable mutt of a dog.

I would like to say that I journeyed toward emotional health and maturity with encouragement from the kindly pharmacist, the kindly soda jerk, the kindly doctor who makes house calls, the kindly cop on the corner, the Good Humor Man, Mr. Rogers, Mr. Green Jeans and Captain Kangaroo, but Brattleboro is not the

Neighborhood of Make-Believe and almost without exception the people who pulled me through my time of need were paid professionals.

Good, kind, committed paid professionals. People whose desire to help was so genuine as to seem either genetic or divinely inspired. Carl Jung said that there is no coming to consciousness without pain. These people helped me to endure the pain. I call them the Angels We Can See.

I was suffering from acute sensitivity to the fact that I had spent the past 30 years of my life circumventing my life, avoiding risk and making counterproductive choices that were more apt to shrink my horizons than widen them. I had been dreaming large within the straits of my small, safe world and all the while feeling deprived of my due, cheated of what I had always felt I deserved or had expected.

My visible angels seemed to know this. They respected the personal history behind my obesity. They saw my anxiety not as a weakness or symptom of decline, but as evidence that something buried alive inside of me was still trying to draw breath. They absorbed the pent-up grief behind my candid, complex replies to the simple question of how are you. They seemed to know that behind the smoke screen of anxiety and purge of tears, empty space awaited.

In retrospect, I know that the emptiness had to be. I was making room for something new, good, real. I had chosen an act more intensive than change—transformation—so that I might say with the poet Rainer Maria Rilke: "And then the knowledge comes to me that I have space within me for a second, timeless, larger life."

I heard, in dread, another voice: *But first you must deal with the space itself.*

7
The Angels We Can See

Y LIST OF VISIBLE ANGELS IS LONG. It begins with
the healers of mind and body: my psychotherapist of 12
years; two other therapists who covered for him whenever he was
away; my GP, Dr. Sczesny; a psychiatrist at the Brattleboro Retreat
recruited by Dr. Sczesny to determine whether I should be taking
antidepressants and if so, persuade me to comply (she said yes, I
said no); the two exercise physiologists at Brattleboro Memorial
Hospital's Cardiac Pulmonary Rehab department, both of whom
I adopted at first sight as the older caring brothers I always wished
I'd had; every good soul at Hotel Pharmacy; my cardiologist Dr.
Tupper, the medical director of the Cardiac Rehab program; the
hospital's diabetes educator who had been monitoring my diabetes since my diagnosis; the hospital's registered dietician; and the
entire staff of doctors, nurses, and technicians in the Emergency
Department.

Also: two charismatic Episcopal priests; a supportive (but un-
dermining), tenderhearted (but demanding) boss; my landlord,
possibly the nicest guy in the world and his family; a nutritionist
who mentored me through a bizarre diet based on my food sensi-
tivities; my acupuncturist of many years with whom I had enjoyed
many philosophical, theological and political discussions; my chiropractor, also of many years, whose sunny temperament made
our visits truly restorative; a naturopath; several tai chi instructors;

two massage therapists, one a radiantly nurturing mother of three and the other a brilliant but often befuddled mother of one daughter, 6 goats, and 10 chickens; a team of exceptionally compassionate physical therapists; a speech therapist who exercised my vocal cords and shared my sympathy for ants; a cranial-sacral practitioner who believed that the Pleiadians had already returned to Earth, or were preparing to.

Also: an enviably tranquil hospice worker who conducted a class called Death and Dying for Beginners, which my therapist made me take, not once, but twice; practitioners of various bodyworking and soul-healing techniques; the whole caring congregation at St. Michael's Episcopal Church and its truly inspired choir and music director; sponsors and fellow members at Overeaters Anonymous; and Buffy, my hair dresser of 12 years, a woman who had adopted a fusion of Catholicism and New Age metaphysics that fueled many long and soulful talks at the salon.

I am indebted to these professionals. Because they made my process so clear to me, I concluded that most of them had experienced their own dark night of the soul. With tact, they helped me to bear mine, work it, and navigate through it.

Some of them have left town, two of them have retired, some I can no longer afford, others I no longer need. But several others remain an important part of my journey and continue to demonstrate the advantage of staying in one place long enough to build a village of one's own.

There was a popular series of TV commercials running at this time that I enjoyed because it captured the comfort and cheer of my visible angels. These commercials feature a reasonably sized, tight-knit, and synchronized crowd of people referred to as the Verizon Network. A diverse and multi-generational group, most of whom are wearing white construction hats, red shirts, and gray pants, they walk the streets night and day, embarked on a seemingly endless mission equipped with laptops, cell phones, metal suitcases, and an air of quiet efficiency and subdued bonhomie.

United, amiable, unstoppable, they appear at opportune moments to assure their customers that they remain digitally connected even in creepy dead zones, standing firm behind a team leader in a blue shirt and glasses who adds a thumbs-up to the words, "You're good!"

The leader of my team would have to be Alec. My therapist. As of this writing we still meet on a weekly basis, which means that we have been meeting for 19 years. He is close to my age, which means that we first met in our forties and now that we are in our sixties, the notion that we have aged together warms me at times and at other times sends a chill down my spine.

I can describe Alec to you. He has a tall, lean body, a kind, generous face and a scrutinizing but sensitive stare. He has kept fit and trim all these years (works out, bikes, runs?), he wears wire-frame glasses (did he wear them 20 years ago?) and still has plenty of hair, once dirty blond, now streaked silver and gray. He sports a neat, sparse beard that's turned white (did he always have that beard?) and although he laughs when appropriate, for the most part he insists on a professional, unnervingly sober manner (what is he *really* thinking?).

I can describe him but I cannot tell you about him. He does not share. Over the years I have deduced that before becoming a certified mental health counselor, he was a Methodist minister and an SIT graduate of the same program in intercultural management I would later administer. I believe he has a family. He must be a man of principle because sometimes his strict nondisclosure policy will give way to a spate of deep political conviction. And because I see him attending events at the annual Brattleboro Literary Festival, I take him to be a serious reader. (A writer perhaps?)

I first started seeing Alec at a time in my life when I found myself as close to the edge as I ever want to be. It was summer. I was 42 years old. I had plunged into a continuous state of unrest and terror, into the grip of staggeringly intense, nonstop panic attacks. I had only a dim understanding of my issues at the time and of the tools available for controlling and changing my thoughts. I felt victimized. The energy raging through my body and psyche felt random, amorphous, and monstrous. It was my slice of the family curse, something I was destined and doomed to endure.

Just before I met Alec, I found some relief in the words of John Page, a soldier and statesman who distinguished himself in early American history as a Virginia Congressman and Governor. Shortly after the publication of the Declaration of Independence, Page wrote to his friend Thomas Jefferson: "Do you not think an angel rides in the whirlwind and directs this storm?"

The answer for me was yes, not only with regard to the preposterous success of the American Revolution but also to my torment. I was being, not tested, but directed. What fetched me back from the brink of collapse again and again was a belief that my guardian angels, the ones we *cannot* see, intended for an empowering calm to come out of the chaos consuming me.

Whipped by the whirlwind of that awful summer, I agreed to a few drugs: elavil, an antidepressant that I tolerated for 2 months because it knocked me into a deep sleep every night within 10 minutes of taking it; inderal, a beta blocker known as the stage fright drug, which I tolerated for 4 months; and valium, which I held on to for awhile.

I took a lot of long, fast walks that summer. I slammed a lot of tennis balls against a concrete wall. I joined organizations that crowded my life with meetings, art openings, readings, writing assignments, and volunteer work because I could not tolerate being home alone. A friend from the old bar crowd with New Age sensibilities re-surfaced and stayed in constant touch. I asked my mother to bring me a teddy bear, which is how I came to have Bear. And I set out to find a new therapist, having reached closure with one in the spring while feeling "cured" and strong.

The fact that I felt peace only when reminded that there were angels riding in my whirlwind persuaded me to investigate a nonprofit organization called the Brattleboro Pastoral Counseling Center. I found the words "pastoral counseling" compelling and I liked the fact that this was non-sectarian pastoral counseling, as I had lost interest in organized religion back in high school. For the past year and a half I had been an atheist. But now I suspected that at least half my anxiety could be traced to my provisional address in a godless universe. I was an atheist but I did not wish to be.

The Brattleboro Pastoral Counseling Center promised meaningful answers to life's problems, a sliding scale fee (I did not have health insurance at the time), and a commitment to helping individuals address their issues within the context of personal faith and values. Surely so much fear, specifically fear and loathing of death, could be managed best by a fusion of psychological and spiritual growth. I liked the fact that Alec had been a minister because the Christ story remained an appealing gateway for me. And I liked the fact that he was a man, which injected piquancy, even competitiveness, into our interaction, a spark, to keep things lively.

You might be wondering, along with my mother, my doctor and numerous other people in my life why, after 2 decades of therapy, I am not fixed yet. I don't know.

Maybe it's because I don't go there to be cured, but to be witnessed. Alec is a constant in my life, one of the few. I sit on his couch and tell him stories; maybe the story of my life is an open-ended, unceasing process and that's why we have not reached closure. Maybe not. Maybe my life ends abruptly with death. We talk about that, too. Maybe it's because in pastoral counseling, the underlying presumption is that life's challenges are not problems in need of fixing so much as portals to a greater understanding of things mortal and immortal, and such conversations could go on forever.

Maybe when the conventional treatment for mental illness shifted preponderantly to psychoactive drugs, which can be dispensed and monitored by psychiatrists in outpatient settings, psychotherapists dodged extinction by assimilating life coaching skills into their practice. Certainly over the years Alec has advised me on matters I would not associate with psychoanalysis or even cognitive behavioral therapy.

I have come to value and trust his tips on how to manage my finances, stay out of debt, and negotiate with credit card companies, how to deal with the bureaucracy of social services and the Vermont Department of Labor, how to conduct myself in a professional setting and give a good job interview. Over the years his counseling has included topics as diverse as the fully human nature of Christ, the virtues of a Wallace Stegner novel, the madness of Republicans, what to do if you're driving and you see a tornado up ahead, tricks for ridding your home of mice, and a correct calorie count on what I had for lunch that day.

I respect the fact that we have stuck with each other. He has not given up on me and I have not given up on him. I have friends who hop from one therapist to another, letting months, sometimes years go by between hops. Or they might turn the process over to body workers or psychics. Or they might slip back into old patterns and bad habits when change and inner conflict carry too far down to the bone. Talk therapy does not work for everyone. But I had made a commitment to Alec, just as I had made a commitment to the 1200-page trilogy I was in the midst of writing, and together, the book and I longed for positive growth. And fruition.

I also experienced comfort and grace in the fact that because we had stuck it out, when I found myself in the abyss again, Alec was already there. Things were in place when I had my heart attack. He knew what he needed to know.

He knew better than I did why, on the occasion of my first visit since my hospitalization, when faced with climbing the three flights of steep stairs to his office in the First Baptist Church on Main Street, I feared against all reason that the exertion would overtax my diseased heart. He would know why I took it slow and why I worried all the way up *against all reason* that I would get to the top step and drop dead at his feet.

He would know why. But he might not tell me. Not for years.

If Alec was familiar, Jeff and Casey were a revelation. It sounds absurd but until I met Jeff and Casey, I had never thought that men could be kind. Genuinely, purely kind. Humane, yes, and men could be generous and they could be charitable, friendly, even compassionate, but not kind. This was a quality that I encountered again and again whenever I reported to the Cardiac and Pulmonary Rehab Department at Brattleboro Memorial Hospital.

I still do. Although its nationally certified Cardiac Rehabilitation Program only lasts 12 weeks, the hospital offers a maintenance program for graduates. I have kept a membership at the local gym and have since added bicycling and swimming to my exercise routine, but I still go to Cardio Rehab at the hospital every Monday, Wednesday, and Friday. I go to work out, check my pulse and blood pressure, and bask in the smart, laid-back, good-natured, good-humored care that only Jeff and Casey can provide.

When I first met Jeff, I cried. I cried because the fact that I was sitting there talking to somebody with the title "Cardiac Coordinator" about participating in something called the "Cardiac Rehabilitation Program" meant one of two things, or both: that I had failed to take proper care of myself and that I was dying or fated to die before my time.

Halfway through our intake interview, I found myself weeping for a third reason. As soon as we started talking, with Jeff asking questions and me answering in between nose blows—what brought you to the ER, what procedure did you have, have there been any symptoms since, what impact has "the event" had on your life—I felt becalmed.

As he added professional footnotes to my personal data—my risk factors, previous health history, medications, activity level—I experienced hope.

As we wrapped things up—occupation, leisure pursuits, living situation, height and weight—I found comfort in the prospect that here was a person big enough, patient enough, hardy and sane enough to absorb the fear that had turned me into a wrecked soul overnight. I must have asked him 30 times that day if I was going to be all right and even though he kept saying yes, I have asked him *30,000* times since.

Imagine my joy when I discovered that there were two of him. Jeff had an assistant: a physical therapist named Casey. In a program that includes people recovering from heart attacks, heart surgery, angina or stenting, even while spelling out the actions necessary to avoiding future cardiac events, neither one of them allows his patients to feel sick or helpless.

Although I hated, dreaded, and wept through my first rehab class, I formed the impression that through the sheer alchemy of Jeff and Casey's personalities, I was going to leave each session feeling like a whole and healthy being and that through a combination of risk factor modification, education, exercise and group support, bolstered by the robust humor and kindness of my teachers, I had a good chance of becoming even more so.

The heart is a muscle, it needs to be exercised, and it can be trained.

Jeff was 41 when I met him. He was born in Elkins, West Virginia (population 7,000), and raised in Moorefield (population 2,500). To my ears, his West Virginia twang sounds Southern at times, at other times Western and at all times soothingly down to earth.

He was married when I met him (no children, five dogs), now divorced (his wife got the dogs). He loves sports, running, and hiking and he dreams of one day doing nothing but travel. Where would he go? Everywhere. He is big and tall, soft, and round about the edges with a bit of a gut that he keeps reining in, a shiny shaved head and a face in which the eager, hopeful boy he once was is still endearingly evident. He is not boyish, however. He is virile and grounded, a gentle bear of a man with a booming voice and an open and openhearted manner.

Casey, by contrast, is a fox, lean and wiry with a bit of an edge, sharp features and a gravelly, almost grating voice. He was in his mid-forties when I met him, and thriving. He had come a long way from Santa Ana and Los Angeles, where he grew up with severe dyslexia, a vindictive alcoholic stepfather and seven stepsiblings, five of whom were headed for lives in and out of jail. Casey went to college instead, Landmark College in Putney, Vermont, one of the few institutions of higher education designed for students who learn differently.

Married to a professor of nursing, with one daughter, he is a devout bicycle rider who has raced bikes on both coasts and in Europe and coached the Women's Yale Cycling Team. He currently commutes to work on an old Royal Enfield motorcycle that he refurbished and restored. He sails. He coaches the girls' soccer team at the local high school, builds his own boats and furniture, and bakes his own bread in a wood-fired oven.

Jeff reflects and philosophizes. Casey analyzes and thinks. Jeff's sense of humor is broad, his energy flowing. Casey's humor is sharp, his energy clipped. They both love motorcycles, own them, ride them, take road trips on them, and hone their skills at track days in Loudon, New Hampshire.

At my first rehab class, I received a three-ring binder filled with photocopied articles, charts, and black-and-white illustrations. Only the Traditional Healthy Mediterranean Diet Pyramid was in color. This notebook was supplementary information, good, basic, useful stuff that I never even glanced at until months after the class had ended.

Reading the first six sections—Risk Factors, Angina and Heart Disease, Anatomy and Physiology, Cardiac Procedures, Pharmacy, Advanced Directives—would have confirmed that I really did have coronary artery disease. It was the same fearful thinking that prevented me from reading the information sheets the pharmacy had handed out with the drugs I was taking, the worry that reading about a heart attack would bring one on.

The seventh section of the notebook, Emotional Aspects of Heart Disease, seemed less intimidating and I gave it a glance or two. It helped me to read that recovering cardiac patients become hyper-aware of the slightest discomfort in the chest. So I'm not the only one. "Fleeting sensations can trigger a fear that something awful is about to happen." Great. I'm not as crazy as I thought. "This is normal and should gradually disappear." Well. When?

I would have appreciated a more extensive Emotional Aspect section. If there was anything they needed to know about the impact of a diagnosis of coronary artery disease, all they had to do was ask me. Actually, they wouldn't even have to ask; I had no qualms about telling them exactly what I was thinking or feeling. And that is where Jeff and Casey showed extraordinary patience, humor, and tact.

The final seven sections in the notebook—Stress Management, Exercise and the Environment, CPR, Smoking, Nutrition, Dr. Dean Ornish's Program and Recipes—I already knew about. I had already stocked up on all the Dean Ornish books. There wasn't much they could tell me, certainly not about the importance of stress management, exercise, and nutrition.

Yes, I had smoked until just a month previous and yes, I was still a thistle of raw nerves, but I was sitting in a classroom with people who had never heard of tempeh, seitan, edamame, miso, spelt or even Egg Beaters, people who considered tofu, sprouts, and hummus repulsive and blue corn chips and rice cakes a joke, people who referred to whole grain items as cardboard and used the word granola only when referring to the crunch heads who actually ate this crap.

I was way ahead of these guys, thanks to my mother. She had fed us healthy, home-cooked meals that always included a green vegetable and a fresh salad. She maintained her figure through five pregnancies. In the early 1970s, as she approached her fiftieth birthday, she started doing yoga. She stopped eating meat. She developed a diet around whole grains, yogurt, bean curd, fresh fish, and vegetables. We started making fun of her. Our Mother the Hippie. At 50.

One day, after finishing a Sun Salutation that left us tittering, she said, "Look. Some women my age would go out and have an affair. I'm doing this instead." Which shut us up but good.

After moving to Vermont, once I had quit the late night grab-and-go meals incidental to making theatre and the late-night salty snacks incidental to working in smoke-choked bars, I started gravitating toward the health food stores. By the time I landed in a cardio-rehab class at Brattleboro Memorial, I knew all about soy milk and rice milk, hemp and kombucha, couscous, quinoa, wheat berries, teff, and kamu.

My attitude toward the rehab classes dangled between denial— I don't really belong here. Do I? I'm not sick, not really, right? — and catastrophizing—this pain, this tingling, another heart attack, yes? The big one?

I obsessed over the question: Heart attack or indigestion? (Coroners frequently find rolls of antacid in the pockets of heart attack victims.) How do I know, how do I *know*, at three o'clock in the morning, whether I should take a Tums or drive myself to the ER? (Casey: "Martha, if you think you're having a heart attack, you call 911. You don't get in a car and drive yourself anywhere.")

Each rehab class consisted of an hour of education and an hour in the fitness room hooked up to a heart monitor. Hospital staff members made guest appearances to conduct the classes on nutrition, diabetes, hypertension, and medications. Outsiders offered instruction in tai chi, stress management, healthy eating, and advanced directives. Jeff and Casey handled the classes on risk factors, cholesterol, anatomy and physiology, organic labeling, the psychology of mindless eating, fraudulent food marketing, and exercise.

It was good to be with other people whose experiences resembled mine and whose concerns appeared to be similar, although I discovered that not many people were as willing as I to divulge their wild, logically flawed fears. I felt grateful when I met people with conditions more grievous than mine. I felt superior when I spotted the ones who would never quit smoking or stop consuming junk. I felt inspired by the patients in their eighties who showed up feisty, fully dressed and in their right minds to walk the treadmills and crack wise when asked about their symptoms.

I had to leave work in the middle of the day to attend all 36 classes but I never missed a single one, thanks to a boss who held an Ed.D degree from Harvard in education and public health, which naturally inclined her to support my wellness initiative. Also I never missed a class because I needed to be rescued again and again from my all-devouring anxiety by the white cardiac knights of Brattleboro Memorial whose motto shall be, "No you're not dying, shut up and keep walking."

During one of my early trips to the emergency department for an episode of SVT tachycardia, I asked them to call Jeff at Cardio-Rehab. He happened to be available and when he arrived, I bombarded him with questions.

How long is this terror going to go on, when will I feel safe again, when will I start to trust my body, why do I keep going into rapid heart beat, is there something wrong with my heart, am I dying or will I die before my time?

"How, *how*, am I going to get through this?"

Jeff took my hand in a gesture that had both friendliness and authority in it and said, "By knowing that you're going to be all right."

Alec, Jeff, and Casey. Creating new voices for me to hear and to heed. About who I was and what was important and how I was going to keep on making it better.

And Michele.

Archangel. Best friend. Fifteen years younger than me, five foot two, with gentle brown eyes, luxuriant dark brown hair, and an uncommonly pretty face.

At the time of my heart attack, we were single, childless women who lived alone without family nearby. She had just broken up with her boyfriend—again—and was feeling as lost as I was. She lived right down the road now. Throughout that first bleak, bottomless winter, on more evenings than either of us care to remember, Michele trekked over in the cold and the dark after dinner so we could sit together on my couch and watch endless reruns of *Friends* (her favorite sitcom) and *Frasier* (mine).

We each had our own version of a broken heart. We were not drinkers or druggies. We were trying not to eat. We talked. We shared our stories, aired out our fears, let loose our tears and pictured our best lives: mine as a successfully published writer, hers as married and secure, settled in a clean country house, with a doting partner, happy children, healthy pets, and a lifestyle consistent with her vegetarian and humanist values.

For now, we became each other's *person*. Emergency contact. Mender of household appliances and broken hearts. The ride to the train station or the mechanic. The run to the drugstore for a prescription or new thermometer, the bringer of soup, saltine crackers, and ginger ale. Slayer of internalized negative voices. Friday night date. The phone call, the cri de coeur any time of day or night.

I never called her at work and I never called her at four o'clock in the morning, but just knowing that I could helped. At twilight, when I found myself in a spin, she would be Right There. In my house, at my side, making tea, making popcorn, calm and steady, yanking me back from the vortical edge.

One way or another, she was there. She taught me what it meant to be a friend.

8
If Jesus Came to My House

*I*F *JESUS CAME TO MY HOUSE* is a children's book by Joan
Gale Thomas that has been reissued 19 times since its publication in 1951. I remember the book primarily because we, my siblings and I, thought it was hilarious. The very idea. A little boy, age
5 or 6, wonders what it would be like if Jesus dropped in for the afternoon, rather casually as it turns out, unannounced, unattended,
and the same age as he. He is beardless, of course, barefoot, and
dressed in a short biblical robe that shows his spindly legs. A plain
halo around his head is the only clue to his identity.

Politeness abounds as the boy narrator entertains the boy Jesus.
He imagines making tea and offering his rocking chair in front of
the fire, giving his guest a tour of the nicest rooms in the house,
showing him his favorite toys and giving him the best one, taking
him out to the garden to pick flowers and gather apples while birds
assemble on cue and sing for joy.

After showing his barefoot guest the corner in the hall where
the shadows at night frighten him and realizing that Jesus will not
be staying to keep him from being afraid, the narrator finds comfort
in knowing that he can go to the Lord's house whenever he wants
and he can do for others what he would have done for Jesus.

I fear that my siblings and I missed the point. We focused on
the mismatch between the proceedings and the occasion, on the
casual dress, the commonplace activities, and informal relations

with the Son of God. Jesus' parting words, "Thank you for a lovely afternoon," never failed to rock us with laughter.

Religion was important in our house but not paramount. Emphasis was placed on advancing ourselves in this world, not the next. For my father, intellectual pursuits mattered most because getting into heaven mattered not half so much as getting into a good school. It was how *he* had turned out so well.

Vincent Paul Moravec was the eldest son of Croatian and Slovenian immigrants who came through Ellis Island in the early years of the twentieth century. He had been raised Catholic, very. My mother, the issue of an English, Scots-Irish, Pennsylvania Dutch, we-arrived-shortly-after-the-Mayflower family, had been raised Presbyterian. Very. Her maternal grandfather, the Reverend John Raymond Mohr, had been pastor at Presbyterian churches in Rural Valley and Freedom, Pennsylvania.

My father abandoned Catholicism during WWII, when an aerial torpedo hit and sank his destroyer in the Mediterranean Sea. Although he managed to save himself and several of his shipmates by keeping them afloat until they were picked up a day later by another destroyer, I remember him saying that while his ship went down, he watched his mates hold up pictures of their families and cry out for their wives.

He said, "I couldn't believe anymore in a God who would let things like that happen." It was the only time I ever heard him speak of his war experience.

When my parents married at King's Chapel in Boston, with an Anglican priest officiating, all my grandparents questioned the couple's ability to co-exist. They were not the only ones. My father was captain of the Harvard football team. One night during dinner at the Harvard Varsity Club, his teammate and good buddy Robert F. Kennedy nearly brought him to tears by insisting that he was going to hell because he had married a Protestant.

After hours of debate, when it became clear that my father was not going to agree that his marriage had damned him to perdition, Bobby put in a late-night phone call to Archbishop Cushing for a judgment. No doubt my father was relieved when the future cardinal replied, "It all depends."

I have no idea how their different indoctrinations affected my parents' marriage, but when they started having children, they began looking for a religion that a Presbyterian and a Catholic, however lapsed, could tolerate. They found their compromise in the Episcopal Church.

The Episcopal faith is often referred to as Catholic Lite or Catholicism without the guilt. It has retained its roots in the beginning of Christianity and kept the splendor of processionals, clerical costume, rites, and music while forgoing confession, the adoration of Mary, celibacy for its priests, purgatory, and the pope. Women are eligible for ordination, sacraments are not denied to divorced persons, and issues like birth control are considered a matter of "personal informed conscience."

In the 1960s, both my father and I stopped attending church. He stopped because the Episcopal Church appeared to be taking a sharp left turn toward activism, advocacy, and progressive thought. Some of its leaders started weighing in on civil rights and the Vietnam War. My father believed the separation of church and state ought to work both ways.

Me? I was in high school. The Beatles had discovered sitars and Transcendental Meditation[R]. I had discovered Freud's *Civilization and Its Discontents*, which compared religion to childhood neurosis.

After my summer in the whirlwind, the summer I walked into Alec's office at the Pastoral Counseling Center, I started sampling different churches in town. I saved St. Michael's Episcopal for last because it felt inevitable. It also happened to be the most welcoming of all the churches I had tried. The Baptist and Congregational "blue hairs" clearly disapproved of my informal dress. Episcopalians don't care what you wear, just as long as you show up.

The Episcopal Church strikes a reasoned balance between traditional liturgical worship and twenty-first century imperatives. Unfortunately, its membership continues to decline amid complaints that it has become too flexible over the interpretation of historic Christianity; too friendly to other faiths, too accommodating to people who are gay, lesbian, bisexual and/or transgender; and too interested in secular political causes to properly sustain its ministry, creeds, and sacraments.

Not a problem for me. The mission at St. Michael's is stated thus: "We believe that God's love is unconditional. We welcome all people and we affirm the worth, dignity and gifts of every person as a beloved child of God." Communion, too, is open: "In our celebration of the Eucharist, there is no one here who is ineligible or unwelcome, no one who has too many doubts or too few beliefs."

This was a church that I could believe in. Now if I could only believe in God.

At the time of my heart attack, St. Michael's was in the care of two extraordinary priests: Thomas, our Rector, a gay man in his late twenties with the charisma of a rock star; and Jean, our Priest Associate, a divorced woman of keen intellect in her seventies, a mother of four, and a recovering alcoholic.

Although I had already been a member of the congregation for 5 years, I found new directions in both Thomas and Jean. When I needed sustenance beyond therapy and medicine, I turned to the priests. I argued and questioned and dared them to prove the existence of God. I hoped that one day one of them would say something awesome enough to turn on the light inside.

They had an impossible task. My body, my soul, my life, and whole being ached. Thomas said of me that he had never met anyone who wanted so much to believe. And yet I went on refusing. Whenever he started talking about Christ, his miracles, his divinity, his affiliation with the Holy Ghost and God, as though it were all true, I tilted my head at him and asked, "Do you really believe this crap?"

"Absolutely. I do." His eyes would look directly and searchingly into mine. "Without question, without doubt."

I loved his faith. I loved being around it. I loved feeding off of it. Boy-faced and blond, Thomas was one of the most fully present, genuine and completely attractive people I had ever known. He was a very young man, and short, but he had vast presence and a grand charm. The word charisma had been created for people like him.

After a year and a half as our rector, Thomas married Tom, an older, much taller man who had once served as the pastor at the United Methodist Church in town. To celebrate their union, Thomas and Tom invited the whole of St. Michael's to a festive reception in the undercroft late one Sunday afternoon. As I drove to the reception, I worried. Would it be well attended? Or would our staid, mostly older parishioners choose this occasion to show their true feelings about their practicing, self-avowed gay priest by not turning out?

When I arrived and found the undercroft packed, I nearly wept. The whole congregation was there.

So I belonged to a good church full of good people, a church whose members could not have too many doubts and whose numbers were swelling in response to a convergence of the events of September 11, 2001, and the magnetic draw of its new priest. The problem was me, my war with God, the conflict between my unbelief and my insatiable hunger for meaning.

I did not believe in a personal, petitionable God, despite the fact that I talked to him constantly. When you live alone, often on the edge of madness, you have to talk to *somebody.* Ninety-five percent of the time, I felt certain there was no one listening or registering concern. I found the absence 150 percent unbearable. On the other hand, I refused to commit to a loving God for no other reason than to make myself feel better.

Wishful thinking was not enough. *Belief* was not enough. I had to *know.*

I attended church most Sundays. Church helped relieve my anxiety, especially when we sang an old familiar hymn and I wept or when the choir performed a sublime piece of music—something by Bach or William Billings, a spiritual or an African folk song— and I wept—or when the words of a sermon hit home.

I sat in the back, always in the back, in the last pew right next to the door, which not only indirectly expressed my lack of commitment but also provided me with a quick escape should I feel the need to run screaming from a nave full of people who actually believed what they were hearing, singing, and saying. Sometimes I found myself believing, which accounted for the outbreaks of tears, sometimes I remained aloof and discerning, and at other times I experienced unbelief to the point of contempt.

There were more plausible religious teachings. Taoism struck me as more accurate and true, Buddhism as more sane and more sensible, Hinduism as more satisfying, Unitarianism as more free-thinking. It wasn't too long after returning to the Church that I realized I could never in all honesty believe or belong.

Was I ready to give away all my worldly possessions? No. Did I love my neighbor as myself? Not really. Until I could deny myself and take up my cross daily, until I could show the charity of the Good Samaritan and the forgivingness of a crucified man, I could only be an Aspiring Christian.

Nietzsche said, "There has been only one Christian—and he died on the cross."

I attended church so that I might sing. I attended church so that I might experience an uplift in the music and ritual illuminating the stories being told. I went to be part of a community, to meet in joy or in grief and find a divine construct in the stories of our lives. I attended church to receive support from that community in times of doubt, personal hardship, or fear for the world's fate. I attended church because I had read enough articles about the heightened immune systems, lowered blood pressure, and increased longevity of regular churchgoers.

But I resisted. One day, during Communion, the congregation was asked to remain seated and sing, "We Are Climbing Jacob's Ladder." We sang softly and fell into a mindless, singsong cadence. After one verse, I stopped and looked around because suddenly I felt the nonsense draining out of me.

Although surrounded by intelligent, informed, mature adults, I could see only children.

We are climbing Jacob's ladder. The woman in front of me, a woman in her early seventies with the straight bangs and bowl cut of a little girl looked like just that. Her eyes were milky soft;

her face was upturned, her expression daft, hurt and dumb. *We are climbing Jacob's ladder.* Her fingers were splayed flat on the pew, her legs crossed at the ankles. And then with wet, lovestruck eyes, she started rocking back and forth to the rhythmic flow of the song. *We are climbing Jacob's ladder.* She was rocking, not in the way of a woman cradling a child, but of a child being cradled. *Soldiers of the cross.*

I wanted to pick her up and throw her like a ragdoll across the room. I felt furious, superior, repulsed. If ever I were going to run screaming from the madness of believers, this would have been the time.

This is what we are, I thought, this is all we are, children, terrified children whistling in the dark. Lost in immeasurable space, we yearn against all reason and material evidence for a Father who will punish and protect because in our infantilism and our dementia we want life to be fair and life to be just and life to go on forever. We come to church to resurrect our model parent, take our placebo in the form of a flavorless wafer and find succor in our pretty little story of Christ.

When I said these words to Thomas one day, he looked indignant. "Excuse me? But this is *not* a pretty little story. Stonings, beheadings? Doubt and betrayal, torture, excruciating death on a cross? There is nothing pretty about it."

Good point.

I did on occasion come close to the inner circle of belief, just close enough to start feeling grounded, centered, and connected, close enough to imagine that I was a being with a soul and that we were all souls-in-one, until I tripped yet again on a remembrance of things dead and fell into the black hole at the center of it all.

The God I did not believe in I despised. I did not despise him because he allowed bad things to happen to good people. I never expected God to be Santa Claus, keeping track of who was naughty and nice. I did not despise him because his biblical self was at best inconsistent. It wasn't his fault he couldn't keep his own story straight. The Bible was not his story, but man's. No. I despised God because of death.

Death was the worst idea anybody ever thought of. The cruelest joke, the cruelest master, a pitiless, psychotic beast. Murderer. The seed of human misery and mother of all religion, a natural process, perhaps, but the worse thing ever. Death was wrong, absolutely completely horribly shockingly wrong.

It was the unacceptable thing a piece of chocolate cake was meant to fix.

In midlife when I began to search in earnest for the source of my obesity, I found myself churning up memories of a pediatrician who preyed on naked children, a movie about an oversized ape, and a concept of death as annihilation.

When I was 4, there was a window in my bedroom set high inside the vee made by a sloped ceiling. At dusk, my mother tucked me in. We told each other what we had done that day, sometimes she read a story, then she kissed me and turned out the light.

She left. I was fine. I gazed up at the window and watched without fear while the crepuscular blue turned to star-flecked black. It was a beautiful sight, a beautiful world, inside and out. I was fine. We were all fine. Everything was fine. Until my brother made me watch *King Kong*. Those eyes. Those enormous, molesting eyes peering through the window, destroying the peace and privacy of my world.

After that, the enchanted view from my room became a chasm. After that, when my mother switched off the light and left, I turned my head away from what had become an abyss, from just the chance of seeing the mad, abusing eyes of the beast. Nothing was fine after that.

Then, after hearing that at death people went away and never came back, the abyss entered my room and swallowed me whole, devastating my ego night after night with sensations of my own nonbeing. Which is supposed to be impossible. I disagree.

Others ask: how can you be afraid of Nothing?

Nothing is the fear.

The world went on. The Soviets successfully tested a hydrogen bomb and launched Sputnik into orbit. A-Bomb tests, mushroom clouds, U-2 spy planes, nuclear submarines, space race, arms race, proxy wars, Bay of Pigs. President Kennedy asked for increased military spending and told the American people to start building fallout shelters. The construction of the Berlin Wall, the Cuban Missile Crisis, Vietnam, the Middle East. First strike. Massive retaliation.

I was 12 years old and dragging my mother out of bed in the middle of the night. What is the meaning of it all? If nothing endures, why bother to go on? Why live? Why live as though we matter? *How* can we live if we don't believe we do?

The soul was a tale told by the brain. Extinction inevitable. Significance nil. I sometimes wonder if eating became my way of saying *but I am alive.*

One day, while seated in Thomas's office, I started weeping uncontrollably for my deceased cat. Thomas attempted to console me by reading aloud the last paragraph of James Joyce's short story *The Dead*. I have no idea whether Thomas tries to console all his bereft parishioners with these words, but he was smart enough to know that a paragraph of breathtaking writing, a paragraph considered to be some of the finest lines ever written in the English language, would stir something within me.

It didn't make things better or more clear, but when the reader's attention shifts from snow falling faintly on a churchyard to snow falling faintly through the universe, something opened up, something greater than me, something that miraculously took its meaning from my longing to be inside of it, in touch with it, in tune.

But why Christianity?

Because of Christ.

He is here. He is here now. He stands at my side. To the right of me and a little bit behind, like a person ready to take hold of my elbow and steer me across the street. For years that is what I called him, The Man at My Elbow, because I felt too skeptical and too squeamish to call him Jesus.

But I knew him right off. It was 7 years before my heart attack. It was Christmas Eve, as a matter of fact, but it was one of those years when I just wasn't feeling it. I was seated in church for the evening service, waiting to take Communion. I kept looking at my watch to calculate how much of *It's a Wonderful Life* would still be on TV when I got home. I had seen it a gazillion times, and I owned it, of course, but this was Christmas Eve and it was my only way of observing the occasion.

I was going home to an empty house, a house that would be dark until I arrived to turn on the lights, an apartment without a tree, without a fireplace, without children, in-laws or presents. I had nothing on for Christmas Day. Friends were either out of town or simply not thinking of me. As for family, I sometimes preferred the purgatory of being home alone at Christmas to the twin stresses of travel and dysfunctional negative reinforcement.

So this was my holiday: A Christmas Eve dinner of grilled rib eye steak, potato gratin with Gruyere, and fresh greens with blue cheese, church at nine o'clock, then the last 45 minutes of *It's a Wonderful Life*, while eating a chocolate mousse bombe from the gourmet Country Deli.

The success of spending Christmas alone depended on a refrigerator stuffed with pastries, roasts and pate, smoked fish and Stilton cheese.

It was one of those years when I had nothing to do and nowhere to go and an overstocked pantry and fridge. I must have been feeling sorry for myself, too sorry to be transported by the pageantry playing out before me, the incense, the candles, the carols and song. I wasn't feeling close to God or even conscious of Christ, in fact I was feeling rather bored, when suddenly—he was there. To the right of me and just a little bit behind.

A presence. A distinct presence. Something good, very. And Other, outside of me. If it were made manifest, it would be radiance. Made of everlasting stuff. Some One. I felt the thrill of recognition. I whispered, "Jesus, is that you?"

He answered, "Yes."

That was all he said. And that's all there was to it. One minute there was nobody there. And the next minute, He was.

He didn't say much else. What he wanted me to know, all I

needed to know, apparently, was this: I will always be with you. I am always here.

For years, I pretty much ignored him. Occasionally I wondered about him but I kept brushing him off. What I could not shake, however, was the notion that I had to keep brushing him off because he was still there. I did not encourage him. But he remained. I did not believe in him, not really. He was my 6-foot rabbit, the ultimate imaginary friend.

He was just The Man at My Elbow. A distant point of light, really, a glint of vital energy that occasionally took shape in my mind as a man who bore some resemblance to depictions of Jesus, most closely to Rembrandt's famously humanizing Heads of Christ.

And then one morning, a year after my heart attack, something persuaded me to think that Jesus really had come to my house.

I was getting ready for work. Since I was still living on the edge, I had awakened exhausted and worried that life would feel impossible before I even got out of bed. Sure enough. The moment I sat up, I felt a fresh rush of adrenaline rocket through my gut, which promised another day of sitting in the office disguising my efforts to contain cyclonic fits of dread.

I heard a voice. "There is nothing to fear."

He had spoken. He had also moved, because the voice sounded to the left of me and Jesus always sits on my right. (Sits, stands, floats, shines, whatever, lately he dances a lot.) But it came from outside of me, this voice, *it was not me,* and suddenly I believed that maybe, just maybe, there was nothing to fear, and that was when the healing began.

9
Deep Breath Baby Step

One doesn't discover new lands without consenting to lose sight of the shore for a very long time.

—ANDRÉ GIDE

I HAD FALLEN HALF ASLEEP just living my life, which, at the time of my heart attack, meant adjusting to a new job with some staggering challenges. My surprise visit to the hospital reawakened issues that had lain dormant for some time. I understood almost at once that these issues could not be lulled back to their quiescent state, not this time. They could not be stuffed back down, my body told me so, my hypervigilant gut.

The issues were clear. First, I was growing old fast and fiercely aware that possibilities were not endless anymore, that I had come nowhere near to achieving my goals in life and that it wasn't only time that was running out, but also energy and perfect health.

Second, I had tumbled into another prolonged episode of severe anxiety attacks, caused chiefly by a panic disorder, and to a lesser degree, agoraphobia, specific phobias and probably generalized anxiety disorder as well. Alec never named what ailed me. It seemed to be part of his strategy.

Third, I may have just quit tobacco but I was still numbing myself with emotional eating, compulsive spending, physical withdrawal from the world, channel surfing, and repeated viewings of favorite movies. I continued to rely on phobias to keep me "safe," anxiety to distract me from feeling my feelings, and fantasies to protect me from real despair.

Fourth, I was determined that life should have meaning and life should be joyful, not fearful, and that I should experience connection to a God in whom I had no faith.

Here be dragons—aging, anxiety, addiction, and agnosticism— tempests that had fogged the horizon for years but that needed to clear off now if life was going to make sense again or be enjoyed or, at the very least, appreciated in all its ambiguity. My soul had set sail aboard a fleet of four ships laden with mystery, and for the moment, I could imagine only a murky, perpetual drift between two points, losing sight of the shore and falling off at the edge of the sea.

> *Feelings come and go like clouds in a windy sky.*
> *Conscious breathing is my anchor.*
> —THICH NHAT HANH

One of the first most helpful things I learned was how to breathe correctly.

Chronic indigestion, acid reflux, a natural tendency to hyperventilate, and 40 years of tobacco use had made my respiratory tract susceptible to the shallow, confused breathing that comes with, causes, or results from anxiety.

Jeff and Casey devoted a whole Cardio-Rehab class to diaphragmatic breathing. It is simple. As you inhale, expand your abdomen and pull the air into your lungs with as little movement from your chest as possible. As you exhale, flatten your abdomen, pulling your navel in toward your spine so as to empty out completely, like a balloon releasing air. Breathe through your nose: rhythmically, deeply, effortlessly.

On the inhale and exhale, they suggested we say to ourselves, "Breathing in, I calm my body. Breathing out, I release all tension." (Thich Nhat Hanh says, "Breathing out, I smile."). We were encouraged to develop our own magic words. Breathe in love, peace, and joy. Breathe out fear, worry, and negativity. Anger. Grief. Guilt and shame. Betrayal, abandonment, rejection, neglect. Ghosts.

Within a month I began to notice a difference. For me, one of the chief symptoms of anxiety has always been a weird suspicion that I am trying to leave my body. I feel caught up in some accident of levitation, where, capriciously roused by magnetic or aerodynamic forces, my life's breath floats up out of my core, collects into a mad flutter in my chest, and threatens to blast out of the top of my head for destinations mystic and unknown. Abdominal breathing helps.

I don't know yet whether my oversensitive gut is a blessing as well as a curse. We all have the enteric nervous system embedded in the lining of our gastrointestinal tracts, a system found to be so extensive and complex that it is now referred to by some scientists as the second brain.

Anyone who has had a gut feeling, butterflies in the stomach, or the shits knows something about the communication and cooperation that occurs or should occur between the *brain* brain and the brain in the bowel. Although not capable of conscious thought or decision-making, the second brain can operate on its own without connection to the central nervous system or input from the first brain and may one day offer new pathways for regulating behavior and treating stress-related disorders.

I was not surprised to learn that signals from the network of neural circuitry, neurotransmitters, and proteins in my stomach can influence my emotional processing. You know the saying, it's all in your head? For me, it's all my gut.

To say I have a nervous stomach that experiences intolerance for spicy foods and revulsion at the thought of eating calf's brain, chicken butt, and rooster balls does not do justice to the sensitivity of my gut. When there is a perception or an observation, an impression made or a feeling to be felt, all 100 million neurons said to be residing in my second brain feel it first.

My gut is where the stress hormones come into play, where

cortisol pools and percolates, where adrenaline pitches electro-chemical fits before, during, and after an anxiety attack.

My gut is the sump for toxic sludge, where all my unexpressed concerns seep through, rising up as intestinal gas to agitate my breathing or soul vapors to disrupt my powers of thought. It is the idiot judge that mistakes panic for a heart attack, stroke, or nervous collapse. It is the body part girded by the abdominal fat that char-acterizes life-threatening metabolic syndrome.

My gut weighs me down. It is where the tears come from, the drawn-out sobs. It is the fear that clenches. When I feel hurt, it is the part of me that hurts first and most.

My gut is where food is digested, or not, and where feelings are digested. Or not. And while it is controlling the movement and ab-sorption of food, measuring acids and salts, it is channeling waste. It pesters me with muscular contractions and awareness of my in-sipid, material self. It absorbs the energy churning upward from my genitals into my innermost being until I can't tell the difference between spiritual longing and sexual desire. It is the visceral wall that comes apart when personal boundaries are not kept.

It is where embryos should have grown into babies. And in be-tween times, it's the belly that should have been flat.

It is the place where the bottom falls out. The seat of intoler-able loneliness. The portal to the void.

It is also my core. Traditional Chinese medicine places the body's center of gravity three finger widths below and two fin-ger widths behind the navel. This is where the chi is stored, in the lower dan tien, the cinnabar field valued by ancient Taoists intent on transforming the base matter of life into the gold elixir of im-mortality. It is considered the focal point for body awareness and a rooted stance, the energy center vital to breathing, meditation, and the martial arts.

So gut can also be salvation: balance. It is the key to physical and emotional stability. It is where the creative juices flow when I am working well. It is the sun-drenched peace that settles over my stomach during moments of fulfillment and content. It is the safe and cozy place of *me*. And somewhere in all of that, there is a font, a source, God. He must be. Where else?

Everything seemed to burst forth from the same spot, the consternation as well as the calm, the panic as well as the bliss. And so every morning before work, I breathed with my belly to establish my base. And occasionally it happened that when I was not feeling scattered or crazed, when I was not dithering between fight or flight and pumping out adrenaline, when *gut* became *core,* I began to feel centered, grounded, and connected.

I had no clear idea as to how I would become whole and well. I only knew where to begin.

Just breathe.

> *I have been through some terrible things in my life, some of which actually happened.*
>
> —MARK TWAIN

Until my mid-thirties, I thought my suffering was unique and my dysfunctionality a corollary of the "family curse." Somehow I kept missing the fact that I shared a bona fide mental illness with 40 million other Americans.

Even within my family, anxiety was not identified as such and therefore not addressed, because by the time it could no longer be ignored, it had escalated into a temper tantrum, a psychosis, a manic high, or a spectacular nervous breakdown. Anxiety was small-time. Besides, remember? I was the healthy one. The strong one.

Outside of the family, I never had a chance to share or compare my war stories because more often than not I found myself in a college, theatre or restaurant setting, where most people were too busy anesthetizing themselves with alcohol and drugs to reflect upon their reasons for doing so.

It might have helped if I could have attributed my phobias to something more workable than a mysterious, Gothic-sounding insanity in the family. But it *had* to be mysterious, you see. Poor parenting could *not* be the reason we had failed to turn out like the Breckenridges, our emotionally stable, over-achieving and beautifully behaved neighbors in Princeton that my mother insisted we be more like.

As a family, we had shared a series of charming children's books written by Margaret Sidney from 1881 to 1916 called *The Five Little Peppers and How They Grew.*

Another family, closer to us in time and temperament, was *The Happy Hollisters,* by Andrew E Svenson writing as Jerry West. There were five of them, too, with the same age gaps as ours, five rambunctious children prone to exclaiming things like jeepers, zowie, and yikes as they piled into their woodie station wagon and rode off to solve mysteries at locales with names like Lizard Cove, Circus Island, and Pony Hill Farm.

When it became clear that we were distinguishable from the Breckenridges, glaringly so, when the nostalgic glow suffusing the Five Little Peppers and the Happy Hollisters faded to a wistful glimmer, when our behaviors and ambitions began to deviate from the examples set by the prelapsarian families of 1950s' sitcoms, the Cleavers and the Andersons, the Nelsons and the Stones, a reason had to be found. Sense had to be made of what appeared to be preposterous failure.

After my sister's first suicide attempt at age 13, my father speculated that she had inherited a tendency to be morose from her Slavic forebears. He recalled his parents telling him how in the old country life was harsh and the general mood morose until a wedding or feast day offered an occasion for the whole village to cut loose. The celebration carried on for days. People ate and drank and danced until they collapsed, at which point, after sleeping it off, they became morose again.

When my two younger brothers began to break down in ways that rendered the functionality of the Happy Hollisters surreal and the melancholic Slavic temperament an increasingly feeble excuse, my mother introduced the phrase "chemical imbalance" into the family narrative.

My sister and two younger brothers suffered from misfiring synapses and defective circuitry. We called them wacky brain waves. Prolonged fits of weeping and manic delusions were things that happened without apparent cause and existed beyond our control and understanding. And yet they could be fixed—easily—by the antidepressants, antipsychotics, and mood stabilizers that had been sweeping through the mental health field since Thorazine[R] but that now proliferated and prevailed to the point of closing down mental health hospitals and rendering psychoanalysis nearly obsolete.

As a psychiatric social worker at the Buffalo Psychiatric Center in the 1970s, my mother must have seized upon this trend to frame mental illness in strictly biomedical terms as a godsend. In the nick of time, the psycho-pharmacological revolution supplied her with guilt-free mothering.

For the next 25 years she and I clashed over whether nature or nurture stood behind the family curse. Even from the beginning, as frightened as I was by the hospitalizations and doping of my younger siblings, I saw their breakdowns more as a result of faulty parenting than biological illness. I worried that they were not being encouraged to reflect on the origin and meaning of their feelings or instructed in nonchemical ways to manage them.

My mother's insistence that genetics accounted for the failure of her children to live up to their potential had encumbered me with the fear that one day I would succumb to fate and finally slip over the edge. Her insistence had another even sadder unintended effect. My reluctance to perpetuate the curse and saddle myself with dependents whose behavior might resemble what I had witnessed in my siblings played a large part in the fact that I never seriously considered having children of my own.

As the strong and healthy one, I learned to manage my anxiety with talk therapy and upkeep on my diary, a strong faith in holistic health, the martial arts, church, and the rooting rituals of small town life. That was on a conscious level. Unconsciously, I managed my anxiety with the unhealthful habits that my midlife wake-up call had compelled me to discard at last. The addictive behaviors had contained my denial so well that when I finally said "no more!" weeks, months, years would pass before the surge of symptoms released by my heart attack subsided. For longer than I could have imagined, the symptoms remained in full force.

First among the symptoms were the physical furies, the insomnia, the wild fright and illegible scribbling in the middle of the night, the stupefying rushes of adrenaline, the onset of severe colitis, the SVT tachycardia that necessitated trips to the ER, the acute sensitivity to bodily signals, the hypochondria, the continuous need for reassurance as to the state of my health and refusal to be consoled, the inability to feel safe no matter how many times or by whom reassurance was given.

Second among the symptoms were the limitations on my ability to act in the world. They were the fears that made me reluctant to travel beyond my comfort zone, which extended no farther south than Northampton, Massachusetts, and no farther north than Hanover, New Hampshire, a 60-mile radius. Fears that held me back from pursuing jobs more suited to my potential, making myself attractive to the opposite sex, joining my family at holiday gatherings, and taking vacations. The demoralizing fear of waiting for a thunderstorm or severe weather to strike and not leaving the house until the threat had passed. Fears of going insane or dying before my time, the terrors that siphoned away my energy from solving the real threats to my existence: obesity, diabetes, and heart disease.

Third among the symptoms was the existential, purely subjective state of unease. It was the obsession with an unknown or uncertain future, the inability to stop thinking about something once it's perceived as a threat, the toil of a brain in perpetual motion geared to a state of high alert. The endless loop of worst-case scenarios and manufacture of strategies to avoid them, the feelings of inadequacy, the fixation on death.

My heart attack had unleashed these demons in the middle of a cold winter, at the beginning of a new job, in late midlife. They had been let loose before and I had dealt with them all, so why was it happening again? What was wrong with me that I had not yet learned my life lessons?

Layers, I think. The will to heal has layers. I was not repeating myself. I had hit another parallel layer, deeper, more deeply etched than all previous strata and more intense because this time, time itself was running out. It was now or never.

Alec did not encourage me to think in now-or-never terms. For him, the quest did not end. The search for self-actualization, for God, for sense and for meaning can, if we are open, crop up on our deathbeds. And beyond. According to Alec, I would always have anxiety because I was human and because I was me.

And still, I did not consider medication, beyond Xanax. I never did go over the edge. I was never hospitalized. I took pride in the fact that I appeared to have escaped or outwitted the full brunt of the family affliction.

And even though I arose each day feeling exhausted because I had not slept well or jolted awake by shock waves of fear and foreboding, my preference for resolving my childhood trauma without psychiatric medication remained a point of pride. I remained determined to find other ways.

Not knowing when the dawn will come, I open every door.

—Emily Dickinson

I resurrected tricks from the past. Thought stopping: Wear a rubber band on your left wrist and snap it hard every time a negative thought or a vision of disaster enters your head. Reframing: Once you've stopped the thought, replace it with a more positive interpretation. Repeat this until you've assimilated the notion that a potentially stressful situation can be a challenge, not a threat, perhaps even a gift.

Placing faith in these and other cognitive therapy and behavioral change techniques shows true faith in the power of the mind. While an active imagination can prove perilous around an anxiety disorder, mine has proven to be a blessing as well in its ability to correct negative automatic thoughts and expel ghosts.

At the age of 35, when I started dealing with a repressed memory of sexual abuse by my pediatrician, I reduced his power over me with an image, or rather an auditory cue, culled from an incident in the 1932 kidnapping of the Lindbergh baby. The man chosen by the kidnappers to deliver the ransom money reported hearing someone with a German accent call out, "Hey doctor!" in the Bronx cemetery chosen for the drop-off. The association of a German accent with Nazis and the specter of a child killer gave me the means to address the trauma. I tweaked the words a bit and placed my adversary in my path with the attention grabbing *"Herr doktor!"* while doing spinning back kicks into a heavy bag.

At another time in my life, in a campaign to validate my feelings, I gave identities and names to my emotions. Goody Grief and Nervous Nellie. Phoebe Phobic. Compassion was called Shin. I named anxiety Old Friend. Since it was important that I take my feelings with me everywhere I went, each morning when I left the house, I envisioned rounding up my wee tots, at least 26 of them, and herding them down the stairs into the car like noisy kids.

In the words of my acting professor from college, "If it works, use it."

Post heart attack, regardless of how it might have looked or sounded to others, I drew strength from sources as giddy as Bear and as righteous as James Tiberius Kirk.

Bear connected me to my inner traumatized child by allowing Little Marty to reenact attachment to an imaginary friend. He comforted the long lost part of me. I slept with him tucked under my arm and carried him around the house from the living room to the kitchen and back again.

I brought him with me when my tachycardia required me to go the emergency room. I took him to work. At first I left him in the car all day but his little black-button eyes and steadfast manner made me feel guilty about abandoning him, so I started bringing him to the office and sitting him on my desk.

Naturally, I took him to therapy. Alec sometimes asked, "What does Bear say to that?"

"What do you mean, what does he say?"

"He's sitting right there. What does he have to say about this?"

"He doesn't have anything to say about it, he's a stuffed animal, for Chrissake."

He did not speak. Or have opinions. He was simply there.

When Alec asked me to choose a role model among my personal heroes, I zeroed in on an issue he had recently highlighted when he said: "You will do almost anything to avoid the anxiety of not knowing."

Who better to embolden me than someone who intrepidly goes where no man has gone before? Captain Kirk is fearless and, as he never tires of telling Spock, glad to be human. The image of Kirk walking or energizing into a completely unknown, unpredictable, potentially disastrous situation, of bounding through space—the *void*— with confidence and agile courage made me smile when I needed most to smile and remember what it meant to be fully human and engaged. During this time I could occasionally be heard murmuring "Kirk to Enterprise" or "Phasers on stun" or "Inner space: the final frontier!"

With Alec asking me what Bear would say and telling me to think like Captain Kirk, I sometimes wondered which one of us was nuts.

But anything, anything, if it worked.

A technique that had served well in the past was picturing and befriending versions of myself at different stages in life. Little Marty was me at age 5, Dear Martha at age 13, Silly Girl at 21. We talked. I told them again and again that things were different now.

Alec and I spent a lot of time with Little Marty, 5 years old and on her own. We frequently referred back to my image of her pacing up and down a darkened hallway of the house, pacing but softly, weeping but quietly, her insides lacerated by a panic she had to keep to herself because there was nobody There. Her mother had gone out for the evening but would she return? (No, they never come back. Never? No. Never.)

Little Marty could not say and Little Marty could not ask, even though her father and brother were sitting in the den watching television. As frightened as she was, going into the den was not an option. It was getting dark outside and no one had turned on the lights, not even in the den, where the television emitted a cinder gray, sickly sheen. There was no one and nothing to make her feel safe. There was only that unlit hallway, with the carpet rough beneath her bare feet; there was only that time of day, twilight, when the air turned deep blue and then black; there was only open country outside, with no neighbors for miles in any direction; there was only just me.

Stuck in that hallway. Stuck in my thoughts.

Another technique in cognitive restructuring is to write affirmations on slips of paper and tape them all over the house.

With our thoughts we make the world.

—THE BUDDHA

At the start of the twentieth century, a French psychotherapist named Émile Coué whose practice centered on hypnosis and the power of the imagination became a firm believer in self-mastery through conscious, positive autosuggestion. Convinced that the repetition of certain words could compel the unconscious mind to absorb them and that an intensely focused thought could become reality, he instructed his patients to repeat 20 to 40 times daily, in the morning and at night, "Every day in every way, I am getting better and better."

Coué never claimed to have cured anyone, but rather, to have shown his patients how to cure themselves, which places his writings in the thick of self-help manuals that range from Benjamin Franklin's *Poor Richard's Almanack* (1732) to Dale Carnegie's *How to Win Friends and Influence People* (1937) to Norman Vincent Peale's *The Power of Positive Thinking* (1952) and Rhonda Byrne's *The Secret* (2006).

Coué's idea dovetails not only with the personal growth and empowerment movement, but also with the emerging fields of positive psychology, where treating dysfunction and deviant behavior matters less than helping people thrive by nurturing what is best in themselves, and neuroplasticity, which discredits the belief that the human brain is hardwired in childhood and can actually reorganize itself throughout life by forming new neural connections. We are wired for re-inventing ourselves and born to strive for meaningful lives.

Each weekday morning after my heart attack, the time spent preparing for work became a crowded hour of hurried relaxation. I needed to make myself presentable in ways that had nothing to do with hair, makeup, and dress. Obliged to appear coherent and able and to show up at the office not weeping, I concentrated on reassembling the pieces of my psyche that had flown apart during turbulence in the night or in the 10 minutes between shutting off the buzzer alarm and sitting up in bed.

I began with diaphragmatic breathing exercises followed by 15 minutes of inept meditation. Next, I dedicated myself to the proposition that we are capable of re-grooving our brains with empowering thoughts by creating a mind turf where I felt safe. Physically safe. Not likely to die. At least not any time soon.

For 3 years after my hospitalization, the prospect of going into cardiac arrest preyed on my mind every minute of every day and night. The fiery car crash, the lightning strike, the bridge collapse, the shooting rampage, the exotic dish, medicinal herb or prescription drug with the one ingredient that sends me into anaphylactic shock, the calamity at the nearby nuclear plant, the furnace that explodes in the middle of the night or quietly releases toxic fumes through the heat vents while I sleep, the tractor-trailer truck that careens off the road and crashes into my house, leaving me horribly injured and hanging by my fingernails onto the splintered floorboards of my upstairs bedroom, the plane falling out of the sky, the cataclysmic earthquake that's supposed to wipe out California but wipes out Vermont instead, the breakup of the whole damn planet, converged suddenly into a single threat from within: a defective heart.

Each morning after breath work and meditation, I engaged in rote reading from a burgeoning collection of brochures, pamphlets, newspaper articles, books of daily meditations on nonviolent communication, better health, spiritual healing and stress relief along with printouts from online communities like *Daily OM* (*Nurturing Mind, Body and Spirit*) and *Beliefnet* (*Inspiration. Spirituality. Faith.*).

My stash also included tiny motivational or inspirational gift books people had given me and *The Book of Common Prayer.*

I inculcated myself with an array of wisdom and bromides, universal truths and platitudes about how faith expected life to reveal its goodness or how the key to feeling safe was not finding safe people but becoming confident in my ability to take care of myself or about how special I was, guaranteed to survive and find strength I didn't know I had and grace to endure. I was a spiritual being having a human experience.

Read food labels, park at a distance from your destination and always take the stairs. Soak in a warm bath infused with two cups of apple cider vinegar to clear blocked energy and pull the toxins from your body. Make your favorite childhood meal. Use glove puppets to dramatize your inner conflicts. Trust the thread that ties our life's moments together (it is made of love). Imagine yourself as a soaring kite. Do laundry mindfully. Use colors strategically. Focus on your sense of touch. Be a cloud. Become the sky.

When I joined Overeaters Anonymous, I added their little book *For Today* to my matutinal routine. Every daily observation began with a quote—"There is no ache more deadly than striving to be oneself." (Yevgeniy Vinokurov)—followed by a reflection—"Am I willing to admit, deep down, that I'm like other compulsive overeaters?"—followed by an intention for the day: "I do not have to be afraid that my feelings will blow me away. I can allow myself to feel them, talk about them, write about them, and watch them dissipate. I do not need the false security of overeating."

I said the Serenity Prayer.

When I finished indoctrinating myself with positive thoughts, I set my own intentions for the day by visualizing events—the drive to work, meetings, lunch hour, the interminable afternoon stretch, the conflicts, the grind—and imagining myself handling every situation with cheer and equilibrium, not panic, anger, or pain.

I counted my blessings.

When I started working with a speech therapist in hopes of regaining my voice, I added 10 minutes of voice exercises. When I started physical therapy to treat chronic lower back pain, I added back exercises to strengthen my core. When I learned EFT (Emotional Freedom Techniques), I did tapping, which entails tapping your fingertips on the same energy meridians used in acupuncture while addressing a personal issue with an affirmation of unconditional self-love and acceptance.

I ended every session with the words used in a 2,500-year-old Buddhist meditation on loving-kindness: "May I be filled with loving-kindness. May I be well. May I be peaceful and at ease. May I be happy."

If I had time before breakfast, I did tai chi and then read from one of two books that I treated like Bibles, opening them up to random pages for inspiration: *The Path with Heart* and *When Things Fall Apart*, by Jack Kornfield and Pema Chodron, respectively, both American Buddhists who advise against running away from pain. Pema Chodron suggests that only by exposing ourselves to annihilation may we find what is indestructible in us.

Even so, whenever I awoke in a state of terror in the dead of night, I did not settle my nerves by exposing myself to annihilation. Rather, I switched on a projector in my head and ran a scene I had created for just this occasion in an effort to reprogram my negative explanatory style.

The scene opened with wild cheering and applause from a studio audience. As the the host of a bright, brassy, noisy quiz show called *Basketful of Puppies,* I made my first appearance wrestling 100 rollicking puppies down a long flight of stairs. At the bottom of the steps my co-host awaited me perched on a rickety bicycle, Danny Kaye dressed in khaki shorts and a pith helmet, and together, smiling, twinkling, laughing, we rode off into the English countryside singing "Everything is Tickety-Boo."

This last image comes from a movie called *Merry Andrew,* a musical comedy about a proper prep school teacher who inadvertently runs away to the circus. It was Little Marty's favorite movie. She begged her mother every night to take her to see it again. Presumably its joyous, madcap spirit helped to offset the shock of annihilation experienced in that darkened hallway. When the movie left town, it lived on in a record album that she could sing and dance to as many times as she wished.

For my 55-year-old self, there would be no musical comedy relief, no miracle cure, and no grand cathartic moment. Deep breath baby step, that was the way, one diligent day at a time. No sudden awakening or masterful insight, just pieces of thought—mantras, affirmations, small rituals, visualizations, and prayers—designed to bring balance to my perception of the world and of life itself.

My visible angels were in place. My experiment in cognitive restructuring had begun. The empty spaces had been entered into. At last I verged upon the frame of mind required to face the most hideous demon of all, the addiction greater than fear: food.

> *I am no longer afraid of storms, for I am learning how to sail my own ship.*
>
> —LOUISA MAY ALCOTT

THREE

They lived in a large, gracious house that included a mahogany-paneled butler's pantry and a second dining room for the servants, now ghosts. The pantry and the second dining room were located just off a narrow staircase that led up to the abandoned servant's quarters. At the top of the staircase, there was a smaller room that most likely served as an office for the person who managed the house.

She took that room and made it her own. She added a spindly desk, a lamp, and a chair and found a padlock for the door. She cherished the fact that she could lock the door from the inside and fill the room with characters. Tragedy. Wind-swept moors. She called it the writing room.

Out back, at the end of a spacious lawn, there was an in-ground swimming pool edged on three sides by pine trees. Behind the diving board stood the stone statue of a half-clothed, Grecian woman with a placid, compassionate expression scooping a dove up into her hands. They also had two living rooms, one formal and one just for family, a great hall with a grand piano, a slate-floored solarium and bedrooms with fireplaces, marble-appointed baths, and buzzers for summoning defunct servants that were sometimes triggered by mice.

Their 28 rooms was considered a summer cottage where they lived, a gated community of Gatsby-like mansions developed as a private hunting and fishing reserve by tobacco and Wall Street barons at the beginning of the American Century. The serene glamour of money, the grandeur of the landmark mansions, ranging in style from Gothic Revival to Georgian to Tudor to Queen Anne to Spanish Mission, the surprise ruins of teahouses, pavilions, and arbors scattered throughout the enclave of lakes, woods, and quiet winding roads known as Tuxedo Park, offered an ideal setting for children's games.

She was a member, sometimes the leader, of a gang passing noisily from childhood to adolescence. They roved about in packs playing war, painted and armed with spears like characters from Lord of the Flies. *At night, they played French underground, diving into hedges and ditches from the headlights of approaching Nazi motorcars. Inevitably, their night maneuvers shifted from dodging Jerries to breaking up pajama par-*

ties or spying on Mr. Hollis, the piano teacher, who was rumored to be homosexual, whatever that meant, particularly on the nights when they knew Mr. Falk, their fifth-grade teacher, would be coming to dinner, to see what they could see. They were emerging from their turtle shells, cocoons, and rabbit holes to declare and define themselves to the larger world.

She was 12 and ready to wriggle out of her shell, but she kept getting stuck. She was overweight. Occasionally she put out her head to see what she could see but she always drew it back in. She functioned at a high level—good grades, class president, quite the actress, many friends, interests and gifts—but she continued to gain weight, and she never lost her compulsion to retreat from the world. Into the writing room.

The teasing never stopped.

"Oooh gross. What is it?"

He was almost 14 and already determined that his chief endeavor in life should be the getting of immense wealth. The older brother.

"Gross, what a pig."

He did it only when they were alone.

"What is that—that thing? Oh God, put it out of its misery. It's too fat to live."

He made oinking sounds, snufflings, and hog calls every time she walked into the room. He made faces of horror, disgust, and sham vomiting at the sight of her. He did this incessantly, without exception. When nobody else could hear. In the afternoons when she came home from school and found they were the only ones in the house, she escaped to her writing room and crawled out onto the roof with a box full of Oreo cookies or Girl Scout Thin Mints. She did not crawl back inside until the box was empty.

"How could anything so ugly be related to me? Oh gross. Is it human?"

Relief arrived when he left for Phillips Academy Andover, although he still came home for the holidays. At Easter, he sat by the pool for hours with a reflecting visor propped under his chin in an effort to draw color from an April sun. His prep school buddies were tanning in the Caribbean and he had to keep up appearances. She wondered if he went back and lied to them about having been in Bermuda.

She wrote a story about it, a story that made him a rather sad figure of fun.

She wrote it and then she burned it.

It wouldn't do to leave things lying about. He had found her diary once and led her on a frenzied chase around the house while laughing derisively and reading passages out loud. Yes, she had her own writing room now, and yes, she kept it locked, but still, some things were too painful to be left where even she could find them.

Stories about actual people. And the actual things they did.

10
This Is What We Did

It WAS NEARING MIDNIGHT. I was in the Emergency Room—again—scantily covered by a flimsy hospital gown, fitted with an IV bag and hooked up to a heart monitor. I had gone into rapid heart rate—again—or thought I had—and panicked. Although I had never had an episode before my heart attack, the tachycardia was now occurring regularly and making me a familiar face at the ER, where an intravenous shot of adenosine brought me back to a normal sinus rhythm.

On this particular visit, it turned out that my heart rate was normal. Possibly the tachycardia had converted on my way to the hospital or perhaps my anxiety level had reached such tortuous heights that evening that I had misread my pulse and symptoms. Perhaps I had needed an excuse to be somewhere other than home alone at midnight. My behavior must have been startling in some way because a nurse asked if there was anyone we could call, like maybe my priest, and I suppose I said yes. (Michele was still living in Philadelphia training to be a massage therapist.)

The doctor on duty that night happened to be Brattleboro's only osteopath. He strolled into the room holding a small amber vial in one hand and a glass dropper in the other. "Open your mouth," he said.

"Why?"

"Never mind, just open your mouth."

"What for?"

"Open your mouth."

"Is that Rescue Remedy?" I asked warily, as though he had brought a bottle of nitroglycerin to the party.

"Yes."

"What if I'm allergic to it?"

"You're not allergic."

"Can I still take a Xanax when I get home?"

"If you really want to."

"There's no drug interactions or anything?"

"No. Now open your mouth."

"Are you *sure* I can take a Xanax when I get home? I live alone, you know, I tend to get paranoid."

"You didn't have to tell me."

I finally opened my mouth wide enough to take 4 drops of Rescue Remedy, a blend of 5 of the 38 Bach Flower Essences, which are intended to correct emotional imbalances so the body can get back to the business of healing itself.

The five essences that I had just ingested were: Impatiens, which treats tension and irritability; Star of Bethlehem, which corrects trauma and shock; Rock Rose, which corrects terror and panic; Clematis, which restores the balance between reality and fantasy; and Cherry Plum, which corrects temper tantrums and utter despair and also somehow, don't ask me how, imparts the courage to follow one's path in life.

Even so, I was still a frazzle when Thomas swept into the room with his naturally beatific air, looking fresh, great of heart and absolutely fabulous in a flowing, black, floor-length cape.

Thomas gave me his full attention while I explained how I happened to be in the ER at one o'clock in the morning and then wailed, "What the hell is wrong with me?"

He answered, "Nothing. You are learning a whole new way of being."

I remember feeling so overwhelmed that I was actually thrashing about on the gurney, still hooked up and still in a panic, when I said exactly what I was thinking, however odd. "I'm just trying to stay alive! I'm fighting for my life, I feel like I'm fighting for my *soul!*"

"In a sense, you are. Martha? I'm going to tell you something not many people know about. But when I was 13 years old, I weighed 300 pounds."

Thomas did not follow his revelation with advice on how to lose weight or change my relationship with food. Or with God, for that matter. He just wanted me to know that he understood. He wanted me to know what was possible, with proper support. Most importantly, he had made the connection between my obesity and the fact that I was thrashing about in the ER at one o'clock in the morning doing battle for my soul.

As big as I was, we both knew there was something larger than me, something larger than the destructive messages and survival tactics I had internalized as a child. There was something greater than me, pushing to live *through* me. My anxiety was telling me so.

It was Thomas who said the right thing at the right moment in the right way. He made my obesity the context and the core of my struggle. My belief or unbelief in God became secondary to belief in myself.

I may have been in therapy for most of my adult life, I may have snapped a thousand rubber bands against my wrist, taped affirmations to all the mirrors in the house, and once even tried hypnosis, but I had not yet silenced my ghosts. Most of us have them, utterances in our heads that just won't quit, the misguided things we were told as children, things about ourselves and about the world that resurface in the mental chatter driving us to light up a cigarette or tear into a Twinkie, and in the ingrained criticism, still shaping our life choices and decisions.

My ghosts had weakened over the years. They had been exposed, their exclamations muffled by joyful noises about what I was made of, what I could do and how far I could go. But they had not been laid to rest, these ghosts, which is what ghosts want you to do, lay them to rest once and for all and free their troubled souls.

I envied Thomas for escaping my fate. He may have been fat at 13 but somebody had nurtured him back to a healthy weight before he turned 18. I had not been nurtured, but shamed, as when my mother said she was going to town one Saturday afternoon, and I asked excitedly if I could go with her. Her reply shattered me.

"Oh Martha, no, absolutely not—looking like that? I'd be ashamed to be seen on the street with you!"

I was 13 and very heavy.

"Ooooh gross. What is it? Is it human?"

My big brother. It still pains me to look at black-and-white photos of the two of us, when it still *was* just the two of us: beaming out love and joy in a studio portrait; fitting together in one Adirondack chair and playing with our plastic sand buckets; standing in front of a lake in wet bathing suits with our arms wrapped around each other.

Even after the others came along, as the two eldest we still pulled together, grinning in our Davy Crockett coonskin caps and a little later, our Cub Scout and Brownie uniforms. We were engineers and town planners together, adding water tanks, loading platforms, street lamps, and stores to the Lionel model train layout that circled our Christmas tree every year until we were too old to be entertained by toy people and trains.

We were hunters together, stalking and shooting woodchucks and frogs with Joe's new .22 rifle the summer we rented a house in the Catskills. We were co-conspirators, fiendishly convincing the three younger ones that there were mobs of little green men carousing in the woods, but they hadn't seen one yet because they just weren't looking fast enough.

And then he turned on me.

"What is that—that *thing*?"

How could my mother not have known? How could she not have overheard? Or had she known and kept silent in hopes that his bullying would change my ways? Why did I not tell her? Perhaps I did.

I do know that at this point I was the problem child. Since the insanity in our family had not yet emerged, our ranking seemed to depend on our intelligence quotients and our appearance. My mother's five-foot-four frame was full-figured, leggy, and trim. Five births had not added one ounce to it. (Age would not thicken her, either.) The boys were all lean, and at the time that my weight was getting away from me, my sister was developing a gorgeous shape. Only my six-foot-four father, who had been a superb athlete in his youth, needed to watch his weight as middle age came on. I often heard my mother say that obesity ran in his family.

As for the maternal side of the family, personal appearance had been all-important to my prim, Presbyterian, appropriately dressed grandmother. Emily Howe's daughters, my mother and aunt, were always natty and well groomed and her granddaughters, my sister and me, met expectations on Sundays at least, in our pleated skirts, white gloves, white socks, and patent leather shoes. A neat, clean, tasteful, and becoming appearance was a matter not only of self-respect, but also of respect for those that raised you, for those receiving you and for your station and opportunities in life. It was your duty to reflect well.

Although there was nothing wrong with my intelligence quotient, by the time I hit 13, my appearance had gone from chubby to obese almost overnight. I was a misfit in my family and in my culture. One hot summer day when my grandmother Howe found me sweating profusely following a bike ride, she admonished me with a maxim she must have heard from *her* mother: "Horses sweat. Men perspire. Ladies glow."

And? Yes? So that makes me—a horse?

As for my culture, I developed a 40-inch bust, again almost overnight, at a time when the popular ideal for a young woman was a stick-figured, androgynous waif named Twiggy.

Enough said.

I know that my mother despaired of my weight gain. I know she tried dealing with it but I also know that all her attempts failed. Our first trip to Lane Bryant, the retail-clothing store that catered to plus-sized women and girls, was a grim affair. Her disappointment that we should have to be there at all was palpable. When I came out of the dressing room twirling about in a dress that made me feel beautiful, her deflated air flattened into the words, "No, no. You don't want that one. You want this one."

No I didn't. But it's the one we got.

I remember her taking me to a diet doctor, an idiot with one solution. Diet pills. *Speed*. I remember, when I developed a spot or two of acne, my mother determined to head it off with a trip to the dermatologist, another idiot who blamed my pimples on stress and prescribed Valium. *Valium*.

My best friend at this time was the daughter of a famous Broadway actor and one of 6 siblings who lived in an 80-room mansion that became my second home. They were my second family, her Dad, my other Dad. One day, her oldest brother, who was morphing into a hippie before anyone knew what a hippie was, looked appreciatively at me from across the room and said, "You know what, Martha? If you just lost a little weight, you would be a knock-out."

I believe I literally went up on my toes. All of me, my eyebrows, breasts, nipples, hormones, dignity, and self-esteem, perked up and preened. They were the right words, the magic words. But I never heard such words again. In my house, adored older brothers said things like, "Oh God, what a pig. Is it *human*?" And mothers were ashamed to be seen on the street with me.

I retreated to my writing room. It was an austere, cold, and uncomfortable cell, deliberately so, in support of the fact that its function differed from all other rooms in the house. This one was mine. I did have my own bedroom, a well-appointed one, with its own bath, a fireplace, and an alcove made of bookshelves and a built-in desk where I sometimes sat to write. But the bedroom was visible and very much a part of the house. My writing room was located backstairs, tucked away in the servants' quarters, the unused, unfurnished, barely heated wing. It was where I wrote my first "novel," a profusely illustrated tale not surprisingly set in another country, another time, about a secret world within a secret world.

It was a monastic room where I could reach puberty in peace, suffer in silence, run away in place. I could weep, eat a box of cookies or masturbate without fear of discovery. I could gaze out the window onto a gray, moody autumn day while loneliness and loss quickened into a life force that created human drama. In the tragic, romantic ache that was my writing room, I resolved to sit with paper and pen until I had captured the unutterability of what I longed for and why.

I treasured up legal pads, black marble composition books, leather journals, fountain pens, pencils, and fat erasers. I gave pride of place to the books that made me want to be a writer, *Jane Eyre, Wuthering Heights, A High Wind in Jamaica, All the King's Men, Cry the Beloved Country.* And lean, self-contained, self-reliant *Nancy Drew.*

In the space between deep hurt and deep hunger that was my writing room, I went into hiding to keep the best parts of me alive.

It was where I set in stone one of the most blissful memories of my childhood. Staten Island. St. Patrick's Day. I think I was 9. A freak blizzard shut down the whole city. I spent that day in front of a roaring fire writing in quick succession eleven poems. They poured out of me with astonishing ease. I had never done it before. I never did it again. Despite my age, I was aware that what I had written was competent. I also remember thinking it was the most fun I had ever had and that life would be splendid if I could do this forever and nothing else.

At that same wonderful time, while I was discovering the sanctuary of creative thought and animating my secret, private world with words, I started walling up my world with a compulsion to steal. And to eat.

I remember walking into stores feeling feverish all over, in my brain and my body, braced and poised for the kill, the steal, impatient to see how clever I could be, to see what I could get away with, to take what was not mine. Why? Perhaps because something had been taken from me.

In truth, I had been given much. My golden memories attest to that, memories that continue to shimmer over the dark truths underneath. What Alec calls "This is what we did." As opposed to, "And this is how it felt."

When I was 5, we had a garden. In summer and fall, at the end of the day my mother would say to us, "I think we'll have corn tonight. And green beans." And my brother, sister, and I would scramble outside to fetch them. We had orchards bursting with pears, peaches, apples, and tangled patches of berries, all luscious and there for the taking, to eat on the spot or bring home for pie. We kept chickens. We gathered fresh eggs in the mornings and on most Sunday afternoons, while we watched with varying degrees of delight, distress, and dismay, my father emerged from the coop with an axe in one hand and a disgruntled bird in the other. After it ran headless until it dropped, we scalded and plucked it clean, then turned it over to our mother for roasting.

These are the memories of living close to nature, coming to consciousness in conjunction with the sights, sounds, colors, and seasons of the country, the creepy as well as the picturesque: the slightly sickening sight of my father burning hornworms off the to-mato plants, the slightly nauseating smell of scalded chicken flesh and feather, the sadness of finding splotches of blood in the coop where a weasel had foraged in the night, the violence of the rooster that turned so mean my mother had to stand guard with a broom while we waited for the school bus, the terribleness of snakes, the suspense of watching firemen lead a stable full of horses out of an inferno that could not be brought under control.

On summer days I remember feeling soothed by the incessant buzz of insects and the blended scent of manure, hayseed, and wild thyme in the air while walking to our neighbors' dairy farm to visit the cows, the latest litter of kittens, and rogue pockets of coolness in their cavernous barn. I remember swimming in froggy backyard ponds, exploring the overgrown timber of abandoned paddocks, kennels, and barns, climbing hay bales in the field behind our house, and when the chill set in, bringing in pumpkins, kindling and wood, and collapsing in front of a crackling fire to listen to our father read from *The Hardy Boys.*

In winter there were snow drifts that piled higher than our one-storied house and in sugar weather, there were rides on a horse-drawn sled to our neighbor's sugarhouse, a cupolaed shack hung with rusted farm tools and oily lanterns. The production of maple syrup created a manly air of excitement, a sharp contrast between the cold outside and the scorching heat of the fire boiling off the water in the sap and great plumes of steam that etherealized the owner and his sons while they handed out doughnuts, strong coffee, and sugar on snow.

Excitement took on a new meaning with my father's transfer to New York. Life in the city, in addition to running with the pack on our dead end street, meant taking the Staten Island Ferry that smelled of steamed hot dogs and sauerkraut to the manic world of Manhattan. My parents took us to all the museums, to concerts, ballets, plays, and operas. There were vigorous treks through the Museum of Natural History and the Metropolitan Museum of Art; languorous afternoons and nights with Mantle, Maris, and Yogi Berra at Yankee Stadium; and every year the Ice Capades, the Ringling Brothers Circus at Madison Square Garden, and extravagant stage shows at Radio City Music Hall.

These are the memories of urban pageantry, strolling down Fifth Avenue with my mother, sister, and Aunt Martha in the Easter Parade; sitting up on my Dad's shoulders so as not to miss one drum major baton or promenading turkey in the Macy's Thanksgiving Day Parade; buying roasted chestnuts and hot, oversized pretzels from street vendors; skating at Rockefeller Center; shopping at the big department stores; and gaping at the Christmas lights and dazzling window displays.

For some holidays and summer vacations, we traveled to Beaver, 40 miles northwest of Pittsburgh. My mother had been raised there, my father in nearby Bridgewater, and both sides of the family had stayed put, so going to Beaver meant going home to all the grandparents, 25 cousins, 14 aunts and uncles and assorted distant kin. With its broad, tree-lined streets and gracious houses that offered large, hospitable porches for sitting, Beaver gave us idyllic summers on Main Street and Christmases in Bedford Falls with extended family, neighborly neighbors, and roots.

Meanwhile, back in the city, my parents were coming home after midnight, smartly dressed and smelling of tobacco and drink and carrying Playbills from the latest Broadway smash. These are the memories of affluence and optimism, capped by our trip to Washington in January 1961 when Bobby Kennedy invited the old football gang from Harvard to his brother's inauguration. I remember standing directly across from "Jack" while he delivered his inaugural speech and attending a star-studded party at Bobby's house, Hickory Hill, in McLean, Virginia.

I was only 8, but I sensed extraordinary excitement, something tangible, a subtle but shared thrill in the air. It was everywhere, in the clubby restaurants and the hotel lobbies, in the bustle of the streets, the eloquence of broadcast journalists and the attitude on almost every face: promise. Beneath brilliant sunlight and blue sky, I stood beside my parents during what must have been the quintessential moment of their lives as the presidency fell to one of the shining lights of their own generation, everybody young, beautiful, and shooting for the moon.

It was at this time that I began to steal and to overeat.

I don't know why. I do remember developing a daily ritual one summer. While walking to day camp, I stopped at a corner store to add goodies to the lunch box my mother had prepared. Sometimes I stole them, sometimes I paid. Hostess Twinkies, Ring Dings, Devil Dogs. Fritos and Wise^R Potato Chips. Secret food. *My* food. *My* world. My own safe and sound world of devil's food chocolate frosted crème-filled cakes.

Concerned over the rising crime rate in the city, my father moved us to Tuxedo Park, where the most dangerous moments occurred while being driven home from babysitting gigs by staggeringly drunk husbands. Our glittering lifestyle among the well-to-do widened the gap between This Is What We Did and This is How It Felt. It was the best and the worst of times, a toss-up between living well in the bosom of a large, happy family and managing a deep persistent interior ache.

Suddenly, I was fat. Not just chubby anymore, but fat. It was as though my body had enlarged to accommodate all of my abandoned selves: the infant left alone for hours crying in the dark; Little Marty, haunted by images of King Kong and the Titanic, pacing up and down that empty hallway; the school child upset by the wail of sirens in the city, obsessed with the prospect of World War Three and the whole world's end; and now the obese adolescent tormented by the apparent meaninglessness of life and death, bullied, not by classmates, but within her home; the comfort-less child of parents who were not emotionally connecting; parents who were there, but not *There*.

It was a patchwork of these fractured selves that hid away in the writing room, eating sweets. Chocolate, almost always chocolate. To make up for the emotions that were there, but not There.

Sulking, daydreaming, closing ranks with Nancy Drew, Scout Finch, Holden Caulfield, Captain Yossarian, Heathcliff, and Jane Eyre, longing to sink out of sight into an act of creation and maybe write something clever. And so, live forever.

Because God also was not there.

11
Six Oreo Cookies

DURING MY STAY at the Dartmouth-Hitchcock Medical Center, I got a rude lesson in portion control. I assumed my meals had been designed for an overweight diabetic who had presented with a heart attack, so the lean trays brought to my bedside did not surprise me. Even so, my disappointment over one particular item helped awaken me to the realities of my relationship with food.

After 3 days, the cheerful woman who checked in every morning to discuss the following day's menu announced that I would be allowed to have a hamburger, if I so wished. Did I!

I gave a lot of thought to that hamburger over the next 24 hours. My system was in shock from nicotine withdrawal. It had only just begun to reckon with the reduced rations at meal times and it was nowhere near to fathoming the cessation of my habitual afternoon grazing and nightly chocolate fix.

I rejoiced over the prospect of a fat, juicy burger. Warped by the surreal nature of my circumstance, my brain sidestepped reality to produce a full sensory vision of a fresh-ground beef patty charbroiled to that succulent threshold point between medium rare and medium, topped by a slice of melted Vermont cheddar sprinkled with bits of blue cheese, served on a hearty, multigrained butter-toasted bun with pickle and raw onion.

Of course the perfect burger would include french fries, but even in my bewitched state, I understood fries to be unlikely, so I conjured up sides of classic potato salad and coleslaw. I may even have caught a whiff of hickory-smoked bacon emanating from either the burger or the potato salad, but all of this proved irrelevant when the great moment and the lunch tray arrived bearing a lifeless gray, wizened hamburger the size of a flattened golf ball. Not even a hockey puck. Not even the deck of cards depicted on nutrition guides to represent the prescribed 3-ounce serving for meat, fish, or poultry.

Desperate, I savored every bite. My deprived taste buds transformed a slider-sized, overcooked hamburger served on a papery white bun smeared with mustard from a plastic packet, accompanied by watery coleslaw and an insipid dill pickle into something scrumptious. The illusion did not last. After the feast had vanished like a dream from my plate, I fell into a gloom trying to imagine life without cigarettes and the ultimate burger.

Make a fist. That is the correct measure for a food portion.

My lesson in portion distortion continued on the way home from the hospital, when I offered to buy dinner for the two friends who had picked me up. They chose a restaurant with hearty family fare. I ordered a grilled steak salad. Dressing on the side.

When I saw the amount of food headed my way, I felt elated at first and then sickened. It seemed an astonishing amount of food. There was more food in that one humongous salad bowl than I had consumed in 3 days at Dartmouth-Hitchcock. It was fresh and delicious, but I couldn't have eaten it all in one sitting even if I had wanted to. And I didn't want to. I didn't want to because I knew how life would have to be from now on. I took two-thirds of the salad home.

For the hour and a half that I sat in that restaurant, I felt disconnected from the people around me, people whose single suppers of chowder and stuffed potato skins, country fried chicken and slow roasted ribs, cream gravy and three-cheese sauces, honey-glazed biscuits and quadruple chocolate truffle pie probably contained a full days' worth of calories, 2 days' worth of saturated fat and 3 days' worth of sodium.

I doubted they were thinking of the fact that they lived in a supersized world where a medium bag of movie popcorn had bulked up from 5 cups to 11 cups in 20 years' time, a serving of soda from 6 ounces to 20, a bagel from 3 to 6 inches in diameter, a reckless world where restaurants were serving slabs of meat and sandwiches at well over a pound.

No one appeared to be giving much thought to the fact that if not already, he or she was at risk of becoming one of the 90 million obese Americans courting diabetes, asthma, chronic joint pain, heart disease, and some cancers while racking up 150 billion dollars a year in health care costs.

Having already entered this demographic, I felt overwhelmed and dismayed knowing that when I got home, and for the rest of my life, I would have to give assiduous thought to what and how much I put into my body. Well. I didn't *have* to. It was not necessary for me to surrender cigarettes and sugary and fatty and salty foods—unless I wanted to live to be a hundred. Hell, beyond it. And I did. And I do.

There is nothing better than being alive.

Giving up the foods that harm us can invite rigorous self-examination. Beyond sustaining life and giving pleasure, food fuses with our identities. Just watch people misbehave in restaurants when they feel slighted or deprived, how quickly they can regress to brattiness or outright infancy. Every age of man, every era, culture, country and every region of a country, every faith, family and household, nearly every individual, develops a unique and intimate relationship with food.

In my family, there were two ways of doing things. My mother grew up in Beaver with one brother and one sister in an elegant house in a picturesque neighborhood overlooking the Ohio River.

My father grew up in nearby Bridgewater with eight siblings in a squat, two-bedroom house that was faced on one side by railroad tracks and on the other by a fecund old world garden, which I remember most for action-packed Easter egg hunts amid the garlic, tomatoes, and chickens.

At the Howe house on River Road, dinner was tasty and balanced, nutritious and spare. A roast, a vegetable, and a green salad. Sherry and wine, coffee and a sensible dessert. The dining room possessed a gracious charm with its rich red oriental rug, crystal figurines catching light at the windows, and an heirloom grandfather clock that chimed the Westminster Quarters like Big Ben. The table was set with gold-trimmed dinnerware, antique butter pat plates, water goblets, and silver napkin rings. The family gathering was not about food, but about the setting and the conversation. Topics centered on politics, history, and the state of the world, family gossip and trips to Europe and the Far East.

Meanwhile, over at the Moravec homestead, life was about food and the propagation of children. My Grandma Bubba liked to say that life was best when you could still fit them all beneath one blanket. Overwhelmingly Catholic and heavily influenced by Slavic, Italian, and Greek heritages, my father's side of the family enriched my life with more cousins, aunts, and uncles than I could keep track of. At a family gathering, upon hearing that one of my second cousins was pregnant—again—our Carmelite nun Aunt Tupy scurried through what was already a sizable crowd squealing, "Another one, another one!" That pretty much sums it up.

Bubba's dining room was all about a crucifix, sentimental pictures of the Virgin Mary, a Black Forest cuckoo clock that made us cheer no matter how many times the bird came out, and populous holiday celebrations featuring heaped platters of cold-pressed meats and walnut bread; poppy seed cake; cheese streudel; Russian tea cakes and nut rolls; ham, kielbasa, and roast pork; homemade sauerkraut that lived in a crock in the basement; garlic balls boiled in ham broth; greens wilted with bacon grease; cabbage rolls, split pea soup, pierogies, and stuffed peppers.

My Bubba was always in the kitchen bringing forth food; widowed, plump and fertile, quietly jolly and hugely proud of her proliferating brood, stretching out sheets of dough across the kitchen table and neatly cutting noodles for chicken soup or preparing a fried chicken that to this day can set my cousins raving. Her house smelled of the odors of a hundred thousand meals boiled, baked, steamed, and roasted into the walls.

My father's father worked in the steel mills, his mother scrubbed floors. During the Depression years, they dropped their nine children off at a soup kitchen for a free meal at Thanksgiving, but they themselves never went in. The family lived out of an eternal soup pot, a broth that simmered constantly on the stove, where it alternated between being raided for a meal and being replenished for the next one with meat parts, garden vegetables, and beans.

When he made a success of his life, my father linked his upwardly mobile status with food. For him, a well-stocked refrigerator offered emotional safety and security, especially after my mother convinced him to quit smoking and drinking. In our house the abused substance was meat. We had it almost every night. My father loved finding a butcher wherever we lived and talking shop while ordering fresh sausage and prime cuts of beef.

He rewarded us with meat. A stellar report card or honors award sent him on a mission to find the best strip steak for that week's best child. Once I was out of the house and living on my own, whenever he came to visit, the first thing he did was take me grocery shopping to overstock my kitchen so I should not want. The second thing he did was take me out to dinner. As far as I could see, nothing gave him greater satisfaction.

These were the things he could do for me, the way he took care of me, the things we could share. We also had Beethoven in common, the Sunday *Times* crossword and detective fiction, but food was the linchpin of our times together. Even in his absence. Whenever a brother or sister came to visit me, he sent a check to ensure that we share a good meal.

When my mother discovered yoga and health food midway through life, she stopped eating red meat. Anything that bore its live young. She could be militant about what is now called clean eating and self-righteous in her efforts to convert the people around her. We kids can still get a rise out of each other when presented with a small plate of stuffed mushrooms or a cup of tomato bisque by mimicking her habitual exclamation, "I could make a *whole meal* of this!"

She admitted once that she felt like a born-again something-

or-other whose joy upon finding tofu, flaxseed and portion control had filled her with a missionary zeal to spread the good news.

It must have horrified her to watch her husband wreck his health, and at times the peace between them, with a steady diet of bacon, cold cuts, ribs, and chops. There could be deeply rooted tension over who was eating what in their empty nest. My mother made two separate meals every morning and night, his and hers. They shared a household provisioned for two incompatible diets that defined them, hers being a matter of living well, virtuously, and long, his of living well in quite another sense and clinging to what made him feel safe, successful, and secure.

My father died of heart failure at age 65. As of this writing, my mother is preparing to celebrate her ninetieth birthday.

Food is a conjurer. When I miss my Dad and want to feel close to him, I grill a good steak. When I miss my Bubba, I buy a ham hock and make split pea soup so my kitchen will smell like hers. To reconnect with Grandma Howe, I use her everyday Spode dishware or I make a soft-boiled egg in an eggcup. To call up my childhood in general, I fix what we called Poly-Sausage Stew, a soup of kielbasa, potato, and cabbage that my mother made to nourish my father's memories of home. When I want to conjure my mother? I pour a glass of wine, sauté baby bok choy with garlic and call it a meal.

As a child developing my own pact and rapport with food, I discovered its power to bestow autonomy: this was *my* choice. And escape: this was *my* world. Through the long procession of Oreo cookies, Girl Scout Thin Mints, Ring Dings, Devil Dogs, Yodels and Snickers, the beast evolved from comfort food to magic substance and ultimately to what Alec would call it, the thing standing between me and God.

I often wonder if it was the lure of food that drew me to restaurant work. The bulk buying and storage of food guaranteed that I would never starve. The preparation of meals for others felt familial. It was sociable, life giving, merry. There was always somebody around, as in a family; we ate together, like family; we brought in special fare for the holidays and celebrated notable occasions while gossiping, squabbling, and conducting the soap operas of our lives against a backdrop of a steady stream of guests.

My use and abuse of food did not occur at work but rather at home on my nights off. For much of my life, dinner was not dinner unless it contained a meat, a starch, a veggie, and salad. I often longed for the savings and nutrition found in a bowl of brown rice and broccoli, but it just wasn't in me to make a meal of a side.

Binge-ing involved chocolate cookies or chocolate cake. And milk. These were my trigger foods, the ones that disappeared within 4 hours of being brought into the house.

At one point in my life, I tried controlling my infatuation with chocolate by allotting myself one 6-pack of Oreo cookies every night. With milk. It went on for years, this little game, telling myself that I could pass up a candy bar mid-afternoon or a too-large lunch as long as I knew I'd be having my six postprandial cookies that night.

This was semi-effective for as long as I worked in restaurants, where those subversive devils, the Calories That Don't Count, were limited to the calories consumed on holidays and special occasions. Or to food eaten in the middle of the night. Or popcorn at the movies. Samples at the supermarket. Happy hour snacks. Any food that's free.

When my occupation switched from cooking to office work, the number of miraculously non-caloric foods multiplied. Now there were those magical doughnuts left beside the coffee machine. The muffins and croissants served at staff meetings in the morning and the crackers and cheese in the afternoon. The dish of Hershey's Kisses on somebody's desk. The Chinese takeout and store bought cake for birthdays. Fast food in the vending machine at 3:30 to counteract a drop in blood sugar. Dumplings and dips at receptions after work.

When I stopped cooking professionally, not only did the number of Calories That Don't Count increase, but my interest in the culinary arts intensified. I had been doing café-and-grill type cooking but once I quit, I turned into an armchair foodie. Suddenly I loved reading about food. I loved looking at the expertly posed pictures of food. I loved learning about cooking trends and techniques and familiarizing myself with cuisines and lifestyles from around the world. I started reading the Travel section of the Sunday *Times*. I amassed cookbooks, magazines, and recipes. This was in the mid-1990s, when the TV Food Network was catching on and accumulating an array of celebrity chefs. I often came home from work feeling exhausted, frustrated, and depressed, plopped down in front of the Food Network, and slipped into a trance while friendly, chatty cooks recreated for me the security of coming home to find Mom making dinner again.

I spent a great deal of time and money food shopping and stocking up on faddish ingredients for meals I never made. (Who for?) Of the ten thousand recipes I collected over the years, I probably made fewer than 30. I preferred to improvise. It wasn't about eating. It was the idea of food, the alternate reality it could summon up: a fantasy of the good life, of becoming affluent and sophisticated and one day actually living as an adventurous bon vivant with a gourmet kitchen and the means to travel.

After the heart attack, my focus switched to healthful cooking, the science of food, the psychology of eating, and mind-body nutrition.

Even then, the same skewed logic responsible for the Calories That Don't Count applied to holidays. When I faced a holiday alone, food rescued me. As Thanksgiving, Christmas, or Easter drew near, sometimes even the Fourth of July, I spent more and more time at the co-op and the grocery stores, trolling up and down the aisles, lost in that Muzak-induced supermarket stupor, dazed by the options, slick packaging, and high end specialty products, before selecting and bringing home the kill. But not before stopping off at the Country Deli for raspberry knots and chocolate croissants, a mocha ganache or chocolate mousse cake to pad the empty spaces in my heart.

One Thanksgiving, while a local TV station played a continuous loop of the *Indiana Jones* trilogy (this was before *Crystal Skull*) I worked myself into a meditative state making quick breads and cookies; risottos, roasts, and elaborate side dishes; appetizers, salads and chutneys; a menu that kept me busy the whole day and fed me for a week. It was sad and disgusting. Surely I could have found someone to ask over, an SIT student far from home. Obviously I should have donated the food to the homeless shelter and volunteered to cook and serve at the community supper in town.

But what looked like self-indulgence was more likely self-flagellation: you screwed up your life so now you're going to spend *yet another major holiday alone* engulfed by food that will make you fatter, more cut off from the world and closer to leaving it altogether.

What did food mean to me? Mother, father. And heated disputes between them. Two families. Two cultures. Food's consequence varied, from expressions of bounty and love to the disgrace of obesity to life, health, and premature death.

I latched onto food along the way as my salvation, a choice exemplified by those six Oreo cookies, the substance I depended on to get me safe, sane, and whole through the twilight hour, the loneliest part of the day. When alone, I could not conceive of surviving the night without something chocolate waiting in the wings, something standing in readiness to protect me, validate, comfort, and complete me, usually between eight and nine o'clock.

It was annihilation otherwise. It was being left at the mercy of the 4 degrees of disconnect—the void, the vastness, the ache, the pain—and all the subtle gradations between them, like shades on a color wheel or phases of the moon. Chocolate staved off losses apparently too ravaging to bear. It was my defense against the fear of death, my advantage over death itself.

How could I possibly let it go?

12
Big

W HEN I LOOK AT PHOTOGRAPHY of myself from my twenties and thirties, I find that most of the time I was in pretty good shape, not fat, not like I had been at age 13 when my brother Joe bullied me.

What I was was big. I was five foot ten and broad shouldered. I had a large bust that was well proportioned to my hips and as long as I maintained a properly inflected waist, I had an hourglass figure that could be called curvaceous, voluptuous, statuesque. I received my share of ogling and appreciative looks from men, whistles and catcalls, and sometimes I got howled at, which I enjoyed because it validated something inside of me that had been shamed almost out of existence.

During those times in my life when I was fat, I had to deal with the mortification of being fat in a world that rewarded thin. But even when my weight was within a reasonable range, I was big. And I still had to deal with being big.

No matter how I dressed myself or what I weighed, I was a "big girl."

And smart.

My father's pet name for my mother was "little girl." Sometimes he cajoled us into making fun of how scatterbrained and stupid she could be. Next to his six-foot-four frame, my mother was unquestionably little and she did sometimes exhibit what I would call high spirits but another might call lack of discernment. I also know that my father took pride in her considerable intelligence. Nonetheless, his inclination to belittle her, whether unconsciously or in fondness or in a case of outright verbal abuse, angered me and I became competitive with him from adolescence onward. None of the other kids argued with him as often or as vehemently as I did.

My competitiveness with my father carried over to men in general, who for the most part kept their distance. I could never play dumb. I could never play nice.

No one had taught me how to be a big, smart woman in the world.

In my early twenties, after my paranoid year at Syracuse University, I moved to Middlebury, Vermont, to make my way in an environment that felt sane and safe (where everybody knew my name). After a year of washing dishes and cleaning houses while trying to turn my latest book, an epistolary novel about the American Revolution, into a five-act play, I opted for college again. I was in the midst of applying to Middlebury College when I discovered a school in Putney, in the southeast corner of the state, with a stellar theatre department.

Windham College was one of those small liberal arts colleges that flourished in the 1960s and then dwindled as the war in Vietnam came to an end along with the need for student deferments. Robert Frost attended the groundbreaking ceremony, Pearl S. Buck was a trustee, and John Irving taught there while writing his first novel.

By the time I got there, the school was on the verge of financial collapse but it had a theatre department supervised by three extraordinarily talented men who in the summers elevated our department to a first rate professional repertory company. For 2½ years, I spent most of my life in the fine arts building doing theatre, with a concentration on acting and playwriting, scene design, and the conversion of sets into spectacular bonfires during wild parties at the close of each show.

Windham ran out of money in the middle of one spring semester. We were ordered to vacate our dorm rooms within a week, a most unwelcome turn of events for me because I was having a grand time playing Madame Boniface in the French bedroom farce *Hotel Paradiso* on the main stage while rehearsing the lead role in *The Killing of Sister George* in the studio theatre downstairs.

We were heartbroken. The summer repertory season, however, was already in the works, so we theatre folk stuck around for that and in the fall, when the college re-opened under new administration, we stayed. I did and I didn't. I dropped out because I could not in good conscience ask my father to finance a bankrupt diploma. But I got a job washing dishes at the Putney Inn because I could not leave my gang.

We were in love with ourselves, a bit in love with each other and just finding out what we could do.

For the next 2½ years, I awoke at 5 in the morning, dressed and walked 2 miles to the Putney Inn, where I vacuumed all four dining rooms, cleaned the toilets and urinals and washed dishes through lunch. I punched out at two o'clock and walked back up to the college, where I retained room and board in exchange for managing the theatre box office and publicity. I did this until evening and then attended rehearsals after dinner to help out with costumes, props, and sets.

I maintained this grueling schedule because of Paul, Tom, and John. Our theatre gang as a whole contained overlapping circles within circles and we were a large, gregarious lot that spent a great deal of time together at close quarters. My own magic circle within circles consisted of three young men, all bright-eyed, beautiful, and gifted. With Paul, Tom, and John, I developed richly collaborative relationships rather than competitive ones. A fine energy arose among the four of us, an energy generated by the artistry we inspired in each other and fueled by dreams of glory.

We were passionately platonic. Or platonically passionate.

I was in my mid-twenties when we first met. They were just barely out of their teens. We were a bit like Wendy and the Lost Boys some nights, roaming around campus singing the four part harmonies we had learned in chorus, the sprightly madrigal, "April is in my mistress' face" or the patriotic "Chester" or the somber "When Jesus Wept."

We had our mentors, we had packs of showy, smart, talented people to run with, two fully equipped theatres to play in, worry-free room and board, and an abundance of creative and sexual energy. We soaked up everything we could from our teachers and elders and developed our own talents around each other's complementary gifts.

Paul and Tom formed a singing duo, Tom and John formed a singing duo that evolved into a comedy act, and finally Paul and I started writing musicals. In a spontaneous burst of genius, Paul wrote some brilliant music without any formal training. I wrote the book and lyrics for each show, sure that I had finally found the medium—musical theatre—that encompassed all my capacities and interests.

It was no coincidence that every show we wrote, all of which went immediately into production, had lead roles for John and Tom. Their distinctly different physical types and voice ranges, along with their own inventiveness, often helped Paul and me develop our themes and we four were guided and mentored by Rigsby, the theatre's tech director and set designer who directed most of our shows. He was the man behind the curtain.

We were golden children at a golden time in our lives, and everything we touched turned gold, not only with instant achievement but also with promise and potential. Over the next 5 years, we collaborated on six musicals and eight productions, which were extremely well received at Windham, the Putney School, and then in Brattleboro and Cambridge, Massachusetts.

When I met Paul, Tom and John, I had just ended an affair and buried myself, or a part of myself, inside my head. Tom, with whom I shared a goofy rapport and many personal confidences, was in the process of acknowledging his homosexuality. John, with whom I spent hours engaged in philosophical and metaphysical discussions, was still dating his high school sweetheart, who everyone agreed was the most beautiful woman in southern Vermont. Paul, who was without question my twin soul in life and with whom I had the most honest, good clean fun I have ever had with another human being, was fumbling around from one unrequited love to another.

Tom finally emerged from the closet. John nipped over to Bennington to finish his degree, discovered that a woman could be both beautiful *and* brainy and played the field with gusto until meeting his first wife. Paul found Alice, or rather Alice found Paul, and they married.

Meanwhile, I stayed buried. I could not, or thought I could not, have maintained these dear relationships and be a woman, too. To cultivate my creative soul and dreams, I had to be one of the boys. A delicate balance had to be maintained. The big smart woman had to know her place.

Once, during a work session with Paul, for some reason I began to cry. In a rare display of temper, Paul looked up from the piano and said, "Are you crying? No way. God, I hate that. There's no crying allowed, period."

Several hours later, we were seated at a banquet in the college gymnasium, where Alice had joined us, and where someone had forgotten to turn on the heat. Alice whined about the cold for half an hour before finally bursting into tears. Paul was all ears and all sympathy. He placated her with steaming cups of coffee while I sat bewildered and hurt, staring across the table at an expression of humanity, and femininity, that was apparently forbidden to me.

Another time, while sitting with John in front of a theatre in Cambridge during rehearsal break, I caught the fancy of a young man in a car stopped at a traffic light. He was hanging out the window applauding and chattering in a funny, friendly way and I was content to smile back and be admired. What worried me was John's reaction. There was none. He stopped in mid-sentence, froze up, and stared straight ahead as though nothing of interest was happening. The moment between me and my admirer did not exist. In that context, *I* did not exist.

On another occasion, after Paul and Rigsby met me at the bus station for one of my weekend visits to Boston, I found myself traipsing down the street several paces behind them lugging my heavy suitcase. It never occurred to either one of them, both of them gentlemen, to be a gentleman to me.

I don't know what I was projecting or failing to project, but I seemed to have stumbled into the framework I had grown up with: intellect good. Emotions (and body) bad.

At the end of one summer, following the successful run of our first production in Cambridge, I joined my family at a large, rented country house in Western New York. I brought with me a folder full of interviews and glowing notices, including one from the *Boston Globe,* along with tales about critics and journalists taking me out to lunch and encouraging me to go to New York. I had a plan.

It was time to leave Brattleboro and move to Boston, where Paul and Alice had already relocated, and concentrate on turning the musicals into a career. I was a penniless short-order cook, living from paycheck to paycheck, but I knew that my grandmother Howe held a bit of AT&T stock in my name. I went to the family reunion in Western New York expecting approval and applause from everyone there and intending to ask my grandmother to help finance my move and my prospects in Boston.

Would they not praise me? At dinner, would they not ask about my adventures and plans? Would they not pass around my newspaper clippings with pride?

First up was my father, who took me to task for thinking that I could actually make a go of things. You think you're something special, do you? What makes you think that of all the hundreds of thousands of people who want what you want, that of OUT ALL THOSE PEOPLE—he was yelling at this point—you and your friend will make it? You really think YOU'RE SOMETHING SPECIAL?

I told my father yes, I thought I was something special. But he was yelling and my voice sounded small.

Next came big brother Joe, who was well on his way to assembling his fortune in commercial real estate in Washington, D.C. He had married a debutante and heiress from Pittsburgh. They were making their first house beautiful. Gussie was an interior decorator already much in demand. They were expecting their first child.

Joe took me aside like a patriarch in a melodrama: grave, pompous, with a fine cigar for a prop, and advised me to give up my crazy notion about being a writer. It was time to get serious, time to avert a frustrating, mediocre life as a grill cook trapped forever in low-paying, dead-end jobs. Leave Vermont. Move to a small city, where they paid a living wage. His conclusion: "You could make a nice little life for yourself as an office manager somewhere."

I told him that for me, the mediocre life would be the "nice little life" of an office manager, not of a struggling writer.

Last, it was time to face my grandmother and ask her to turn over my stock. She refused. She said I was wasting my life. I was not doing what I should be doing. I should have finished college, I should have become a teacher, as she had done. It was time to stop fooling around with my silly friends in Vermont and *do* something. Look at Joe and Gussie, now *they* are doing something worthwhile, something really valuable, they've bought their first house, they're expecting their first child.

When I managed to get a word in, I asked what was so extraordinary about buying a house and having a baby, as it was something that millions of people worldwide did every day. Big mistake.

I was a disappointment and a disgrace and not living the life expected of me. And finally, the coup de grâce, the utterance repeated so often within the family circle, it seemed as much a mantra as a mandate: It was time I started making my contribution to the world.

I never said much to my grandmother again. Nor she to me, although she lived another 7 years.

And I never moved to Boston. Although we did one more show there, the old gang eventually broke up and scattered. Paul and I parted ways. I returned to Brattleboro and for the next 14 years carved out a living doing the only thing I felt sure I could do, which was to make myself useful in restaurants.

The big smart woman returned to Brattleboro scared half to death of something, bruised and confused by the impression that people didn't know what to make of her or what to do with her or what was best. If I had been differently sized or less intelligent and ambitious, I might have felt less alone in the world, less feared by the world, less odd.

I returned to Brattleboro, *home,* a stranger to my body, a stranger *in* my body, a self without firm boundaries, a mass of hopes and dreams without autonomy; Brattleboro, where I could feel safe and tread water while trying to sort through the differences between what W. H. Auden called the necessary limitations of our nature and the accidental limitations it is our duty to outgrow.

13
Cold Sesame Noodles
and Ben-Hur

Two weeks after I got home from the Dartmouth-Hitchcock Medical Center, my good buddy Kate called and asked if I wanted to go to a Weight Watchers meeting. Kate had always been lean but she was contending now with the first slow creep of a middle-aged spread. Her husband was too, and while he wouldn't be caught dead at a Weight Watchers meeting, where the customer base is 90 percent female, he would benefit from the points-based meals Kate would learn to prepare.

I had never been to a Weight Watchers meeting. I had only once been on an actual diet. I was not in the habit of weighing myself. For most of my life I had no idea what I weighed and I did not much care. My weight went up and down, not as a result of conscious effort, but as a side effect of what was going on in my life at the time and how I felt about it.

Because I didn't own a car until age 34, I walked everywhere I went, which often meant clocking 6 or 7 miles a day. For 20 years I made my living washing dishes, waiting tables, and cooking in restaurants, which kept me on my feet and moving. As soon as I got a car, I signed up for an aerobics class to make sure I remained active for the sake of good health. A year later, when I started training in tae kwon do, for the sake of a black belt, I prioritized physical fitness.

For 5 years, while cooking nights at the Jolly Butcher, I attended brutal tae kwon do classes twice a week and practiced on my own every Saturday morning at the gym, where I also did cardio and strength training every other day. In the summers I took tennis lessons twice a week and played with friends at least twice more. I eventually added tai chi to my training, and only my admission to Smith College as a nontraditional aged student prevented me from adopting any other action-packed hobbies.

As I approached my fortieth birthday, I was the fittest I had ever been, sore as hell most days, but vigorous and trim. I had two boyfriends, one a black belt in Okinawa Kenpo, the other a tai chi instructor, the first representing 6 years of an on-again off-again entanglement and the second having been a ploy to arouse jealousy in the first during one of our off-again stretches.

I had decided to finish college. I had just started classes at Smith and had successfully applied to the Smith Scholars Program, which allowed highly motivated students to spend their junior and senior years working on a special project. Instead of a major, I declared a novel. I used courses in medieval European and Chinese studies to research it and independent study credits to begin it.

I was doing pretty well, I thought. And then it happened. One summer. The summer I turned 40.

Shortly after my June birthday, both boyfriends left town. They decamped at about the same time, under circumstances that had nothing to do with each other, or with me, for that matter. I was doubly bereft. I was also still grieving for my father, who had died two summers before. The staying heat of early July stirred up a reflexive sense of loss and recalled the trauma of being present when he died.

I started slowing down, imperceptibly at first. I turned lazy, but slowly. It was some time before I realized that I was spending most of my nights off from work sacked out in front of the VCR eating Chinese food and watching *Ben-Hur*.

The dazzling 1959 version of *Ben-Hur*.

Apparently the only way for me to manage a solitary evening was to feast on fried noodles and Chinese mustard, spicy Szechuan dumplings, cold sesame noodles, hot and sour soup, brown rice (not white, never white) and one of the house special entrées. It was fortunate that I worked most nights and that this gluttony for tangerine chicken, crispy pork, or Szechuan beef and Charlton Heston's epic proportions didn't happen very often, but it happened often enough to finally catch my attention.

And there was something else. It was summer, yes, and at the Jolly Butcher I worked behind a sizzling hot grill. Even so, there were times when my body just halted while my brain discharged a warm flush all the way down to my toes. The first time it happened, I turned to the nearest waitress and asked, "Wow, was that a hot flash?"

Whatever these power surges were, while not severe, they were becoming more frequent. I did not find them disruptive so much as vaguely unsettling. It felt eerie at times, and sullen, as if something unhappy was haunting my body.

When I started skipping tae kwon do classes to eat Chinese food and watch *Ben-Hur* until I could have performed it, I went to Planned Parenthood and asked if I could be experiencing menopause. They laughed and said, "Oh no! You are much too young!"

But my body was off. Off-kilter, off-balance. By the middle of the summer, it occurred to me that I had become less active. I found myself watching tennis more often than playing it, I had allowed my membership at the gym to expire, and I was dragging through tae kwon do classes. My body stopped listening to me. It stopped responding to the commands I was giving it. My body just—stopped. It felt as though something sluggish and dense had settled into my core and driven the vitality out of my limbs and life story.

One night, during tae kwon do, I burst into tears for no apparent reason and walked out of the room. The next day, my sensei called and suggested that I not return to class. At least not for a while. I was so crushed and so bewildered by the ice in his tone, that I never returned.

Life was becoming grim. I didn't know it, however, because on my nights off I was having a grand old time, great, cozy fun slurping up cold sesame noodles and losing myself in Lew Wallace's manly yet pious tale of Romans, Arabs, and Jews clashing, colluding, and chariot racing during the time of Christ. There is a reason why *Ben-Hur* won 11 Oscars.

But still.

Twice more I went to Planned Parenthood and asked for the test that would determine whether I was perimenopausal. They refused. They just didn't see the point.

But I knew. I knew it in the trickle or the torrent of tears that burst spontaneously and with scant provocation from an achingly empty gut. At the end of the summer, I experienced another loss. Back when my collaborator Paul and I parted ways, I had taken my share of the musicals, the books and lyrics, to my younger brother, also named Paul, an award-winning composer finishing up at Harvard. My brother and I had rewritten all five musicals, which at that point represented 12 years of creative work and my only means to realizing my dream of becoming something other than a grill cook at the Jolly Butcher.

Then for reasons unknown, my brother lost interest in the musicals and dropped them. There was no discussion about it. He just stopped communicating with me. About anything. Our telephone conversations, which had once bubbled over with exchanges about life, feelings, politics, music, and memories enlivened by jokes and lines from favorite movies had fizzled into monologues on his part, monologues about two and only two aspects of his life, his achievements and his trips. The one-sidedness of our talks assumed that I couldn't possibly be doing anything of interest in Vermont. He was living in Manhattan now and married.

My best brother, who for years had felt free to call me at three o'clock in the morning, weepy, disappointed, at times suicidal, now limited information about himself to his awards, commissions, debuts, and travels. Nothing personal. And nothing genuine. By the end of this bizarre summer, I somehow figured out that the musicals, like our once precious relationship, were a dead issue.

By September I was feeling so listless and played out that I went back to Planned Parenthood and demanded they test me for menopause. I understood by now that I had sufficient reason to feel depressed, having lost a father, two boyfriends, my sensei and dojo, my chief artistic endeavor, my dream, and a powerful sibling bond. Even with all that, I insisted that my body was also experiencing a profoundly fatiguing, fundamental change.

Planned Parenthood consented to the test and called a week later to say, "Guess what, you were right!" A month after that, I had my last period, ever. I was done. And that was a great loss, too. Although having children had never been a priority for me, the option had been snatched from my hands. I went into mourning for the children I would not have. I went into mourning because I was only 40 and far too young to be a crone.

All I had now was my new novel, the one I had started at Smith under the generous guidance of my academic advisor, Elizabeth Harries. At our first meeting, she tried discouraging me from being a writer, because *everyone* wanted to be a writer, but after reading my first few papers for one of her classes, she not only recommended me for the Smith Scholars Program, but also, since she was planning to buy a new computer, *gave* me her old one. My first. She then mentored me through Book One of my novel, which the English Department honored with a prestigious literary prize in my senior year.

The book drew me in. The book, the book, it was all I had. I turned away from the world that had caused me so much grief and channeled all my energy into a relationship that would not fail me. As I developed the story, I began to grasp its scope, the amount of research it would take, and the time I would need to write what was threatening to be a trilogy.

It took me 13 years to complete *The Secret Name of God*. During that time, I graduated *magnum cum laude* from Smith, had a nervous breakdown, started hormone replacement therapy and, because I could not imagine standing on my feet 8 hours a day in my old age, quit the restaurant business.

I found my niche at the School for International Training, where it was discovered that I had a gift for administrative work. However, since I didn't want to be an office administrator any more than I wanted to flip burgers for the rest of my life, and since the musicals had petered out, I did what my mother said I must never do. I placed all my eggs in one basket, the book.

I crawled deep down inside of myself to give it my all. Suddenly it was just me. Me and my book. Cats, cigarettes, food, chocolate and favorite movies, a ton of historical research, my diary, and dreams. And my fat.

I now worked a sedentary job. And a very demanding one. I had spare time and energy only for the book and while I did take frequent, long walks, my physical activity did not keep pace with the pernicious combination of the amount of food I was consuming and the decelerating metabolism of early menopause and middle age.

I recall sitting at my desk late one night writing. I remember leaning back to take a break and feeling something that I had not felt for a long time: a bit of back flab, what women would recognize as the roll of fat that jiggles over the bra strap. I was surprised—Jeez, when did that happen?—*bummer*. I leaned forward and then back again to experience the fact of it, rotated my arm several times, slipped my hand under my shirt, felt for it and pinched. Yeah, it's there all right. Shit.

And then something happened, something odd.

I felt the fat and it was good.

It was as though an old merry friend had returned and nestled in around my shoulder. It felt comfortable, familiar. Mesmerized, I sank down into my chair, into my viscera, hips, buttocks, and thighs, seduced into a perverse act of surrender. My house was silent, dark except for the lamp on my desk, steeped in an atmosphere of cigarette smoke, solitude, repose. And submission.

I was walling myself back up. I had to. I had to stay focused on the book, and I had to keep from being hurt again.

I gained 120 pounds in 15 years. It was probably what put me in the hospital. It was the downward, inward drive that had to be redirected now to save my life. It was the fear and shame I had to overcome in order to get myself to my first Weight Watchers meeting.

Yes, the world could still harm me, hurt and disappoint me, but I wanted to be part of it again.

14
Not Fat, Not Really

I N 1963, a homemaker in Queens saw the connection between sustainable weight loss and emotional support. Making use of a diet developed by the New York Board of Health, she invited her neighbors to come together on a regular basis to share and to care.

Jean Nidetch's neighborhood klatch turned into Weight Watchers, the global fellowship of dieters who meet in person or online for weekly weigh-ins and progress reports, to receive awards and accolades, offer tips and pointers, and shore up their motivation with spirited exchanges of backslapping, commiseration, and empathy.

I never would have gone if Kate hadn't made a party of it. I'm not a joiner! I can't afford it! I don't *believe* in weighing myself, I'm not fat, not really. I'm not one of *them,* I can do this on my own. I'm too embarrassed, too pathetic, too ashamed. I'm too fat! I'll break the scale! It would mean . . . exposure.

I went because it brought Kate and me together. Once the best of friends, we had drifted apart over the years. At Weight Watchers we had fun meeting up and going out afterward, shopping for kitchen scales and pedometers, comparing notes and recipes, but within weeks, once she got the gist of it, Kate dropped out. I stayed for another 2½ months.

I liked Weight Watchers. I liked its support of a nutritionally sound diet with exercise, behavior modification, self-discovery, and team spirit. I liked collecting the program materials. I liked buying the cookbooks and the measuring tools, although I never bought the boxed food. I was too much of a co-op snob for that. (I had to be reminded several times by other members that an item was not inherently low-calorie because it came from a health food store.) I measured and weighed everything I ate. I wrote everything down. It was fun. It was a project. A challenge. I weighed in at meetings, paid close attention to the Leader's topic of the week, and felt motivated by the collective goodwill.

I lost 20 pounds.

And then I stopped.

All those women sitting in the front row, *knitting*. All those homey, homely women, self-deprecating jokes and corny complaints about the dumb husband who can eat whatever he wants and not gain a pound or who really needs it but would never in million years get off his you-know-what to attend a meeting.

I got tired of applauding for people I didn't know and plastering a congratulatory smile across my face when I couldn't have cared less. I got tired of paying $15 every week just to weigh in, a ritual that began to feel competitive and that left me feeling terrorized by digits on a scale. I was spending too much money on booklets and gadgets. I got tired of measuring things and writing things down. It was just too pat, and in the end, too tedious. Too dreary and too dull.

There were other reasons, real reasons, there had to be. Was it too much work? Too much effort? And by the way I already ate healthfully, I already worked out 6 days a week; I wasn't one of *them*, I wasn't fat, *not really*. I could do this on my own. And besides, my new job was making me nuts. I had just stopped smoking after *40 years*. And now I was giving up my daily dose of Diet Coke because my nephew Gene kept sending me links to articles about the perils of aspartame. I would not be deprived of *one more thing*.

Perhaps talking about my weight embarrassed me. I never raised my hand to contribute to those meetings. Or to share. I never said a word. Until joining Weight Watchers I had not chipped in one penny to the 60 billion dollar US weight loss industry.

Because I wasn't fat. Not really.

At my graduation from the Cardiac Rehab program, Jeff and Casey made much of the fact that I had managed to quit smoking and lose 20 pounds simultaneously. With my graduation certificate I received a letter from the staff that finished with the words, "You should be proud of all the changes you have made and we are glad you have chosen to continue with the maintenance program. We want to stress that this is just the beginning, but assure you that the changes will get easier. We feel that you will like the new Martha. It will just take some time to get to know her."

Although I never doubted that, whether by Design or dumb luck, what had happened to me had been a blessing in disguise, this "new Martha" was a stranger. I had faith that there was an angel in this whirlwind but it did not feel good. Not at all. Fear still ruled my world. Nothing felt good. Nothing felt right.

One day Alec asked, "Why should it? The difference between old Martha and new Martha is vast."

Another day, at work I got into a long conversation with one of our trainers. That night she sent me a follow-up email that concluded, "Yes, you may experience a death of your old self as you knew her. That is what is scary. You have had a wake-up call, but there is a silver lining. You are still here and you are about to look at life in a very different way!"

People kept referring to the new me, a new perspective, new life. And yes, I had changed some behaviors. But I had also pitched back into my panic mode, which had placed me in a near constant state of unease and alarm, foreboding and dread, nervous strain and distress. In that sense, there was nothing new about it.

My visible angels were working overtime, Michele, Alec, Thomas and Jean, Jeff, and Casey. I needed to hear it over and over again and then some more and then again and they delivered: You're doing all the right things. You're doing great. You'll be fine.

At about the same time I joined Weight Watchers, I began a 6-week course in Mindfulness Stress Management, where I learned that there were two sources of suffering. The first was resistance to what I was experiencing. The second was wanting my life to be other than what it was.

I knew this already. And so do you. Every Buddhist, life coach, and New Age guru brings it up before concluding that all we have is the present moment. But I was a right customer for hearing it again. I had become expert not only at wanting my life to be other than what it was, but also at wanting life itself to be different, a process that did not include death.

I also heard in stress management class that it was not the trigger that created my stress response, but my interpretation of the trigger. Alec and I had been working on that one for a decade. (Martha. Statistically, how many thunderstorms occur nationwide per year? And how many people are killed by them? Tornadoes? Martha. This is Vermont. Statistically, Vermont gets how many tornadoes per year?)

I had gotten to the point where I could leave my house in the morning despite a forecast for a slight chance of thunderstorms later in the day. But this time the bogeyman was lodged inside of me: it was my health, my heart. This time the risk was of being abducted again and sent without warning to the big bad hospital up north with the big bad doctors who did *procedures* and things. This time the risk was of going directly from a twinge in the chest to sudden death.

Throughout this period, when pressed, Alec assured me that things would get better. He hated doing that because I was supposed to be evolving to the point where I could know this myself without asking. He stressed, however, that I must give up a very dear notion of mine: that the day would dawn when I would awake feeling perfect. I wanted perfect.

No such thing.

My experience at Weight Watchers gave rise to more frequent and more in-depth discussions in therapy about my weight. For years there had always been something else going on. There was always a pinch or a crunch or a critical juncture, the latest financial crisis, existential crisis or spiritual epiphany, the latest soul-mangling encounter with a family member, the outpouring of grief for deceased loved ones (animal and human), the absurdity of hating death, the anguish of not having achieved what I had imagined for myself, the quest for autonomy, meaning, and God in the second half of life. With such goings on, there was little time left over for Alec and me to talk about food.

We had at least established by this time that chocolate was my magic substance. I came home to a cold and empty apartment, I cooked for no one, I went to bed alone. One day I would die. But that was okay. Because every night after dinner or an evening out, I had my six Oreo cookies, my brownies, or piece of chocolate cake.

Once we started talking more readily about food, Alec started slipping the words addiction and addict into our discussion. I chafed every time he used the word. Me? Addicted? No. Because I wasn't *fat*. *Not really.*

Alec gently, patiently, encouraged me to try Overeaters Anonymous (OA). After a year of him prodding and me resisting (I may be obese and overweight but I am not *fat*), I went to my first meeting.

I had no idea what to expect. To understand how clueless I was, you need to know that the Wednesday evening meetings I attended took place at the refectory of the Catholic Church, where the rector was affectionately known for his sweet tooth. When I walked in, the first thing I saw was a stack of treats on the counter next to the coffee machine: homemade brownies, a box of peanut brittle, half an angel's food cake, and a plate of miniature glazed doughnuts. My immediate thought was: How nice! They'll be serving refreshments after the meeting!

If you know anything about Overeaters Anonymous, you know that hell would have frozen over first. And yet every week I found myself sitting in that room trying not to glance at the rotating supply of cupcakes, chocolate chip cookies, candy corn, and black licorice, candy canes, marshmallows and Little Debbies. I finally pointed this out and after that, we found a tablecloth artfully draped over the Very Reverend Father's stash of munchies and goodies.

Overeaters Anonymous is a fellowship of men and women who meet in hope and in confidence to solve a problem they all share: compulsive overeating. OA believes compulsive overeating is a progressive disease that can be arrested. There is little in the way of dietary advice, but a great deal of unconditional love and support.

OA believes that the means to recovery is through inner personal change, a shift that can only be achieved by working the Twelve Steps and Twelve Traditions borrowed verbatim from the Alcoholics Anonymous program. People talked about the Twelve Steps as though they were runes, commandments, or mystic portals to bliss. For me, this was the least appealing aspect of OA, the fact that these cumbersome steps were integral to what I considered its best idea: the belief that one must address the whole person—one's physical, emotional, and spiritual well-being—in order to achieve and maintain abstinence.

Abstinence. In OA, you don't go on a diet. You become abstinent. However, when food is the substance that's being abused, abstinence is not a matter of elimination. We don't have to drink eight martinis every day, but we do have to eat. Most of the women at the weekly meeting I attended (and again, women greatly outnumbered men) had identified their substances as sugar and flour. Abstinence was the banishment of both from their diets.

I attended meetings for a year and a half. But I never raised my hand. If I wanted to share my thoughts with the group, I was expected to preface my comment with the greeting, "Hello, I'm Martha and I'm a compulsive overeater." I could not, would not, say those words. *Because I wasn't, not really*.

I would have been equally loath to say, "Hello, I'm Martha and I have coronary artery disease," or "I have diabetes."

I got tired of hearing what a relief it was to know that we were suffering from a disease, that despite references to defects of character and the need to make amends, we were not at fault. We were plagued by kamikaze impulses we could not control.

I was in the midst of a crisis on the road to self-actualization and still locked in a fierce battle against lighting up a cigarette. It felt counterintuitive for me to think of myself as powerless at this time. As for surrendering to God, you can just imagine how this rankled in the mind of a person who was a believer one day and a barking mad atheist the next.

After a while, I got tired of hearing OA members refer to the "living hell of this disease." I lost patience with the victimization mentality of the recovery movement. Most everyone in my group also attended at least one other support group, if not several: AA meetings, Al-Anon and Nar-Anon meetings, Co-Dependents Anonymous, Narcotics and Gamblers Anonymous. They knew where to find the meetings for men only or for women only or for gay, lesbian, and transgendered individuals. They signed up for regional retreats, workshops, and conventions and participated in the 24-hour holiday thankathons. It was a culture unto itself and apparently addictive.

I could not relate to the stories I heard: When I was a little girl, my father gave me a bag of potato chips, and I sat on them, thinking that by breaking them up, I was making more for me to eat. I couldn't wait for my husband to go to bed so I could raid the refrigerator. I canceled dates in the evening because I felt sick from eating all day. I fell into a pattern where all I could do was eat and then sleep, wake up and eat some more and then go back to sleep, and then wake up and eat again.

Almost everybody had spent at least one night writhing on the bathroom floor asking God for help because they couldn't stop eating even after binge-ing to the point of physical pain. Most everybody had picked food from the garbage. I sometimes felt as if I were watching a reality show, waiting to see who could come up with the most grotesque, tragic, or pitiful model for food addiction.

According to the OA literature, compulsive overeaters have been known to eat food that is burnt, stale, or even rotten. They eat off other people's plates, eat off the floor, and drive for miles late at night to cure a craving. They steal money to buy food, lie about what they've eaten, disconnect the phone, and don't answer the door.

They have disfigured and maimed their bodies. They have destroyed their health and their relationships, isolated themselves, and consented to become figures of ridicule. They attract abusive mates. They contemplate suicide.

It was so easy for me to *not* be one of them.

One day during coffee hour after church, I started talking to a woman with 35 years' experience as a clinical nutritionist. She offered her services as a consultant for a health regimen based on an assessment of my lifestyle and a food sensitivity test. The blood test would identify the inflammatory foods (plus molds, environmental chemicals, medications, food colorings and additives) that were causing negative symptoms, which would then guide us in creating a rotation diet compatible with my body chemistry.

It sounded quite sensible. The regimen included the proper management of food and water; supplements and protein snacks; portion control, exercise, and the stressors in one's life. Participants were advised to add 3,500 steps to their daily total. And to chew. Mindfully chew every bite of food until it was liquid.

When I reported this to my mother, she recalled being told as a child that chewing 32 times before swallowing led to better health. Modern macrobiotics recommends chewing 50 to 100 times. Thich Nhat Hahn says 40.

Mindful eating, with its stress on chewing well, is highly recommended for dieters, especially diabetics and cardiac patients. At the time, however, I was too crazed to eat in a conscious manner because silence is considered the main event. There can be no music in the background; no computer in your face; no book, magazine, or newspaper propped up on the table; and of course, no television, which in my home, usually went on the minute I walked in the door.

The results of my food sensitivity test showed that I would be better off eating no wheat or gluten, no dairy, no rice, and no soy. That seemed harsh. Usually, people who choose to eliminate one food group have alternatives, like brown rice or quinoa pasta if you're not eating wheat, or soy products if you're not eating dairy or dairy products if you're not eating soy, but my forbidden foods included all the substitutes as well. Except for corn. I could have corn.

I spent hours vetting grocery stores and scouring labels to put together a suitable pantry and meal plan. I remember eating loads of corn pasta, corn flakes, corn chex, polenta, popcorn, and an astonishing variety of corn chips. As for anything soy, you can just about lose your mind trying to find a processed food that doesn't include it. You might even find your canned tuna marinating in a soy–protein–based vegetable broth.

My list of permitted and forbidden foods did not make sense. I could have all the turkey I wanted but no chicken or duck. I could have limes but not lemons. Lobster and clams were out, shrimp was borderline, but scallops and oysters were fine. Broccoli and brussels sprouts bad, asparagus and string beans good.

The search for appropriate foods became obsessive. I grew so fixated on what I was or was not putting into my body that I ended up overeating allowable foods simply because they were allowed.

I met with Beth, the nutritionist, every other week and stuck with the diet for 9 months. One of the most optimistic and boosterish people I have ever known, Beth's voice—"You're doing great. I am so proud of you, darling, you're going to be a whole new you."—joined with all the other angelic voices that were instilling in me bit by bit, day by day, in miraculous stages, and without my knowing it, courage.

My OA sponsor was another voice: Joan, a New Age Catholic whose sense of the spiritual was searching and profound. "Of course you're going to feel anxious right now," she'd say. "You're changing your philosophy of living and your anxiety is trying to slow you down."

There it was again. Change. The emergence of new me, new life. Everybody seemed to know it, they could see it happening, they could see it coming, everyone but me. I was still hurting, still blind and spinning in the dark.

Joan called and sent emails. She advised me to go to as many OA meetings as possible. And to attend open Alcoholics Anonymous meetings as well. At night, I should make at least one OA phone call. I should read the first Three Steps. Write. Write about the Steps. Write down my food history. Joan's first memory of food was of her father making popcorn at the stove and when he was unable to find the lid to the pan, she danced around the kitchen trying to catch the popping corn.

She would say, "The way you ate got you where you are today. Let go of the material things in life. Let go of your will. And seek the will of God."

This was a problem. Letting go. My mother told me once that I was the most willful child imaginable. She said I was always wanting something, always demanding something, always asking questions and drawing people's attention to something that had captured mine. ("Look! Look!")

One day when I was 16, I remember my mother scolding me while driving home from the mall, furious about something I had done or wanted to do, I can't recall which. In the middle of her tirade, Frank Sinatra came on the radio singing "My Way."

She got twice more excited and started shouting, "That's it, that's it! That's the problem, you always have to do it your way, don't you? And you always will, won't you? They'll have to put this on your tombstone: I did it my way, I did it my way!"

I don't know what the hell was going on in her life at the time but while she vented her spleen by caterwauling, "I did it my way, I did it my way!" I sat crumpled in the passenger seat feeling miserable and thinking, "Well—how else would I do it?"

This was my problem with Overeaters Anonymous. Or that was what I told myself. I was still trying to get the ground beneath my feet to stop heaving about. I needed my strength and my will, I needed control and at least the illusion that I was doing things my way. One morning, after one of my increasingly frequent hiatuses from OA meetings, Joan called me at work to ask how I was doing, and when I said I was feeling anxious, she replied, "I knew that."

"How?"

"Because you're not facing your addiction."

"How do you know?"

"Because you haven't been coming to meetings."

And eventually I stopped. I stopped because it wasn't working. And neither was the anti-inflammatory diet, which I also tapered off at about the same time.

Weight Watchers, stress management, Overeaters Anonymous, mindful eating, special diets: they had all failed to hold my attention. The 20 pounds I had lost at Weight Watchers crept back. Why? What was I missing? Would I have to start smoking again? And what was all the fuss about anyway? *I wasn't fat.*

Halfway through her OA sponsorship of me, Joan received a diagnosis of stage 4 breast cancer. She was my age. We talked at length about her prospects, her chemotherapy, her trip to Johns Hopkins to try a breakthrough treatment. She sounded almost gracious in her acceptance of the situation, as though she were planning a reception for an honored guest. She lived 3 years, 2 and a half years longer than expected. Her obituary said that she "fought fiercely and surrendered with grace."

One day I asked Alec, "What is the relationship between food and God?"

He answered, "The food is your way of keeping God out."

Let go and let God.

In OA they tell you, "Surrender to your higher power."

In church we pray, "Thy will be done."

In tai chi the teacher says, "Sink" or "Relax."

In therapy the heart says, "Grieve."

Even after so many years in therapy, there must have been one last thing my heart was overlooking, something I had to surrender to or let go of or grieve for, something powerful enough to sustain my denial against all reason, something basic and too dear to give up.

15

The Husband Store

A FTER GRADUATING FROM COLLEGE, my sister Barney
drifted toward Brattleboro in search of a living and a life. My
parents took comfort in knowing that I was close by to keep an eye
on my little sister. Barney's mental illness and antisocial traits had
already made her one of life's walking wounded, or a genuine reb-
el, depending on your point of view—she once referred to people
like herself as canaries in the coal mine—but that is another story.

One day, during one of her visits to Vermont, my mother
made an offer to my sister. A deal. If Barney stopped smoking, my
mother would buy contact lenses for her. Barney agreed, although
after a month she stopped wearing the lenses, never wore them
again, and to this day, still smokes. She rolls her own.

What I remember thinking at the time is that I also wore glasses and I also smoked. And yet my mother did not make me the
same offer. Was it because I was the healthy one? Or the fat one?

I don't remember dwelling on it and I never brought it up, but
I probably felt the same secret hurt I experienced when, as a pre-
pubescent child packed in the car with my siblings approaching a
bridge with a specified weight limit, I heard my father say, "Ooops,
we better stop and let Marty out to lighten the load!"

Everybody laughed.

Elevators, too.

Apparently it made sense to my mother to sweeten Barney's appearance by relieving her of her granny glasses. She was the beautiful one—I remember my father raving once that she could be a model—and I was the hulking one, the sexless one, a spinster in my twenties.

One day my mother told my Windham college roommate that she supposed I would marry late in life, probably a man much older than myself who would need taking care of. My roommate, who was also my best friend at the time and a psychotherapist in the making, reported this to me in a fury. I appreciated my friend's indignation, although I didn't quite understand it. I shrugged and said, "That sounds about right," then walked down to the Putney General Store for my favorite lunch, a bologna sandwich and chocolate milkshake.

On another occasion, my mother speculated that some fellow in the bar where I worked had a crush on Barney. When I said no, that actually he was completely smitten with me, which I knew for a fact from a mutual friend, my mother was not only surprised but also skeptical. I was imagining things.

I was always just imagining things.

For the majority of her years as a parent, my mother smothered me with un-love: strictly conditional acceptance.

One year she roared into town, staked her annual claim to a corner in my living room, and proceeded to conduct her customary inspection of my life choices. I was 30-something, working at the Jolly Butcher, devoting most of my spare time to tae kwon do and tennis and preparing to start Smith College as a commuting, full-scholarship student.

Within 3 hours of her arrival, my mother had determined that my job, my lifestyle, my finances (hair color, apartment, and cat) showed no promise of ever being what they should have been by that time; "that time" being yet another birthday, as she coordinated her yearly visits to Vermont with the pleasant days of mid-June and the anniversary of my birth.

Yes, my cat. ("She's not a very pretty cat, is she? Can't you trade her in for something more appealing?") I don't know. Maybe in her experience as a daughter it had been a treasured family tradition to be weighed and found wanting on one's birthday. Or maybe she needed to justify driving 500 miles just to take me out to dinner by finding support for her assumption that nobody else could possibly be interested in observing the occasion.

In addition to my job, my lifestyle and finances (hair color, apartment, and cat), she found fault with my furniture, my weight, my clothing, my tennis game, my boyfriend (who wasn't there that night), my tae kwon teacher (who happened to stop by for a minute), and my dream of achieving success as a writer.

The final humiliation occurred when I discovered that I was out of money for the week. I had exhausted my funds on beer and champagne for 30 friends who had attended my birthday party the night before. With an addict's utter want of pride, I asked my mother for pocket change so I could run up to the store and fetch a pack of cigarettes. This naturally set off another tirade.

When she was done, my mother tossed a $5 bill at me and, before disappearing behind a newspaper and falling spookily silent for the rest of the evening, offered a single solution to my multiple lapses in life: "You had better go out and get yourself a husband!"

A few days later, when I told this to a friend of mine, my friend chuckled and said, "Yeah, right, Ma. I'll just go on down to the husband store. Pick one out."

The husband store is a marvelous place. It has a huge selection of models to choose from, not just the perfect husband for every woman or man in the world, but a different one for every phase of life.

If I were to have been a child bride, my fate would have been sealed on February 9, 1964, during the *Ed Sullivan Show*, when the Beatles changed my body overnight. I would have raced right down to the husband store to put in my bid for the Paul McCartney model. Then, after a week I would have traded Paul for John, because I never could decide which of the two I liked best. After a month of bliss with John, I'd have swapped him back for Paul, and so forth and so on.

When I was 15, I would have traded Lennon/McCartney for

a gentle hippie. Not a berserking rock star or fiery radical, but an artist and a poet, a subtle revolutionary who played acoustic guitar and looked exactly like my first serious crush, otherwise known around school as the walking orgasm.

Even so, by my senior year in high school, I would have been back at the husband store selecting the Frederic Chopin model, the man responsible for some of the most sublime music ever written. While casting myself as Chopin's lover George Sand, the female author who protested social constraints, particularly the ones that denied women the freedom to live full lives, I immersed myself in the bohemian escapades of the mostly impoverished poets, artists, actors, and musicians who practiced their Romantic idealism outside the pale of conventional society.

By the time I got to college, I didn't care so much about the interests, profession, or personal habits of my next husband. All that mattered, really, was that he look like Al Pacino.

Convention dictated that I should have gone to the husband store only once in my life. The fact that I pictured myself as a repeat customer shows that as far as I can recall, even as a moony teenager I never made a production in my mind of the big white wedding. I dreamed instead about a long string of artistic, intellectual, slightly mad lovers. Should a husband and children happen, I imagined being pleased, but I also suspected that I would have been seriously displeased if they slowed me down or got in the way.

When I think back to that evening in June, back to when I was 30-something, when my mother surpassed even herself with her rapid-fire verbal assault, I feel compassion. (I didn't then. I don't remember feeling much of anything then. And you can bet that when I went up to the corner store for cigarettes, I also picked up a Ring Ding.) Having excoriated nearly every facet of my life, she just sat there reading her newspaper, not speaking and not showing much interest in dinner or in me.

I feel compassion because it occurs to me now that it had only been a year since my father died. My mother had just lost her partner of 43 years, and I am thinking that perhaps the only way she could deal with her feelings was to lambaste a rebellious daughter who gave every appearance of being able to take it.

And I feel compassion for myself, sitting in silence across the room from her, looking dumb and confused, aching inside and longing to show her all my birthday presents from the night before just to prove to her that I had friends, and that I had a life, whether it met her expectations or not.

Several years after my mother's whirlwind fault-finding tour, I found myself wondering why I remained unmarried. Until that point I had been telling myself that I had had the repeated bad luck of meeting men who were incapable of intimacy or commitment. And true, every lover thus far had been a variation of the Bad Boy model, an edgy alcoholic to whom marriage would have been a disaster.

I had reached the age, however, when sheer luck no longer served to explain why I kept bringing home the imposter designer husbands, knockoffs who possessed many of the desirable qualities, but not the real right stuff. They fit the pattern—the artist, the martial artist, the intellectual with advanced cooking and carpentry skills—but it was time to admit that I had been shopping all along in the discontinued, discount section of the husband store.

It occurred to me then that *I* may have been the commitment-phobe. Perhaps my freedom was the most important thing, freedom to write, freedom to be me, freedom to be. I hated being told what to do or what not to do, when, how, or why. I was not willing to make the number of compromises a successful marriage seemed to require and equally reluctant to ask another person, particularly someone I loved, to compromise *his* needs, wants, whims, dreams.

My mother was a well-educated, highly intelligent woman who returned to the work force once all of her children were situated in school. But even though she had had her career outside the home, my father could be a difficult man and there is no denying the challenge of raising five children. She must have made dozens of compromises every day along the way.

I can see her now. Telling the priest when she married in 1946 to delete "obey" from "love, honor and obey." I can hear her. Reciting in a noble, yearning tone the noble verses she had committed to memory in high school. Kipling's *If* and Henley's *Invictus* seemed to be her favorites. She wrote her own poetry. She played guitar and sang traditional folk songs and ditties, from "Black is the Color of My True Love's Hair" to "What Shall We Do with the Drunken Sailor?" She loved the activist folk singer Joan Baez, and I suspect, wanted to be her.

I recall her now creating international evenings for us, one night making a full-on Japanese dinner, which we ate with chopsticks kneeling at the coffee table in the living room, while sipping sake and listening to an album of koto music, another night serving us a Greek meal with ouzo while exhorting us to stand up every 10 minutes and dance to the soundtrack of *Zorba the Greek*.

As a middle-aged woman in Paris, she caught the wary eye of a policeman by walking solo along the Seine playing the harmonica. A free spirit, I think, or a wannabe. I will never forget driving down to Smith for an early orientation and watching my 67-year-old mother put on a Grateful Dead tape (her tape, not mine), whip out two silver-plated spoons from her purse, and clack them against her knee and the palm of her hand, playing spoons and jamming with the Dead all the way down to Northampton.

She loved to travel, and after my father died, she did so rather adventurously, spending much of her seventies touring China, Russia, Macchu Pichu, the Galapagos Islands, Turkey, Israel, and Thailand, cruising Alaska, and visiting my youngest brother Matt when he was teaching in the United Arab Emirates, where she naturally rode a camel with Bedouins. A new boyfriend, a sparkle of a man named Victor, brightened her eighties. And as she approached her nineties, she continued walking laps and swimming three times a week; supporting causes like equal marriage laws, pro-choice, and the legalization of marijuana; and remaining engaged in the cultural, political, and technological workings of the world around her.

What else might she have done, what more does she *think* she might have done or wished for, what does she feel she gave up?

I suspect that a lot of Baby Boomers are the spoiled fruit of haunted parents: fathers whose service in WWII left them with unacknowledged, untreated post-traumatic stress disorder, and mothers who felt stifled or suppressed. I think a great many of us were raised by fathers who struggled with unaccountable rage, anxiety, avoidance or emotional numbing, and gifted mothers who had to measure their self-esteem against magazine ads that showed a man spanking his wife because she hadn't store-tested for fresh coffee.

My mother had had a good full life, and yet at some point along the way she must have toted up the compromises she had put on account during her one and only visit to the husband store. Surely something had been lost. Or a sense of it. Or the fear of it.

I see it now as I look back on that evening in June, when she sat seething behind her newspaper, just as *he* had done, a woman whose buried grief rose to the surface in hurtful, inappropriate ways, just as *his* once had.

Maybe I wasn't married because for me, the ideal husband was the one whose most desirable quality rendered him obsolete.

He had to be the one who would leave me alone to live my own life.

16
And This Is How It Felt

I HAVE A MAGIC MIRROR AT HOME. A good, kind, soft-lit mirror that has mercy on my imperfections. When I look into my good kind mirror, I am able to see fat and yet not see fat. It is a self-preserving trick of the mind that keeps me from believing my own eyes.

For years, in my funhouse glass not only did I not see the fat, I did not see a *body* or the right to exist because in our culture, fat bodies are shunned, so mine was not even there. *I* was not there, as profane a thing as the unreflected undead.

Even with all that had happened post heart attack, I could sit in Weight Watchers and OA meetings, roll my eyes and think, "What the hell am I doing here, I'm not fat, not *really*."

At 300 pounds, how could I deny my obesity?

One day Alec told me. "To say you are fat would mean to finally fully acknowledge the trauma of abandonment."

He may have said it before, but I hadn't heard. Now I did.

Challenging my denial would mean giving up all of my defenses, including my dream of a golden age, a nurturing childhood. I would have to confront the terror Little Marty had felt in that empty hallway and compensate for all the times she had been left behind to figure things out on her own.

I would have to forget the long-ago memories. And I would have to try forgiving the less distant ones, from the family reunion in Western New York when I was pigeonholed as a teacher or office manager to one Christmas in Connecticut 20 years later, when new fresh blows to my dignity revealed that very little had changed. A year before my heart attack, half the family gathered in beautiful, affluent Essex where my brother Paul and his wife were renting a house less than a block away from the historic Griswold Inn.

My life was not very praiseworthy at the time. I had lost my position at SIT and had spent the past year and a half collecting severance pay and then unemployment compensation. I had applied for 80 jobs and interviewed for 35 before finding work taking orders at a maple syrup company, where I was discharged 2 months later for reasons unknown. I was currently living on my mother's good graces. We had agreed that she would keep me afloat while I finished work on another novel, *The Odd Body Vanity Squad*.

I had just received a ludicrously negative critique of Book One of *The Secret Name of God* from an editor at Random House, which hurt terribly but not half so much as the evidence that my beloved cat was dying, although I had not yet allowed the possibility to crystallize in my thoughts.

There was not much to brag or be mirthful about in my life but I was too excited to be spending Christmas with half my family in picture-perfect Essex to be appropriately ashamed of myself.

Once there, I found myself struggling to rise above a deplorable weekend. Our hostess harassed us every 2 hours to help with the dishes and the food prep. People responded waspishly to just about everything I said and Paul presented an excellent albeit unfortunate likeness of Ebenezer Scrooge.

At one point I overheard him telling my 18-year-old nephew, "Look, Gene, you might as well face it. *Life sucks* and the sooner you realize it, the sooner you can decide what you're going to do about it—give up? Or make lemonade."

This was the composer who had just won the Pulitzer Prize in music and whose wife was an editor at a major publishing house with her own imprint and a Newbery Medal and a Printz Award winner among her authors. They were a handsome, successful Manhattan couple and as far as I could see, depressed, or maybe just tragically uncomfortable around family.

Despite the strained air cast by depressing hints that our hosts couldn't wait to see the backs of us, I went on persuading myself that I was having a wonderful time. With my wonderful family. Until the morning after Christmas. While waiting to take Gene and me to the train station, Paul zeroed in on my dysfunctional life.

"Look, face it, Mart, no one is ever going to publish your book. You need to *get a job*."

He said this at least nine times in the course of the conversation. I was living in a fantasy world, just fooling myself, look at you, what are you *doing,* your life is a mess and life is unfair and by the way, nobody is ever *ever* going to publish your book and you have got to *get a job*.

Alec later said that I should have replied, "Gee, Bro, thanks for your support, I really appreciate it," and walked out.

But I was still trying to convince myself that I was having a wonderful time.

The illusion cracked when my nephew Gene, my sister's brilliant boy, my buddy, the closest I'll ever come to having a son, started echoing everything Paul said in what was beginning to look like a horribly inept intervention.

My youngest brother Matt sulked in the background, having never been anointed or inclined to pass judgment on his siblings—this condescension was not in his nature, this invective not in his vocabulary—and knowing from experience how quickly the withering eye could change direction and sweep into unrealized corners of his own existence.

Our hostess, who was making turkey sandwiches for Gene and me to eat on the train, emerged from the kitchen periodically to point out that even if I published a book, I'd be lucky if I made a thousand dollars, so I still needed to *find work*.

"Sure," she said, "we'd all like to have our mothers support us so we can sit around and just write all day, but that's not realistic. You need to *find a job*."

She then implied that I had never had a job in my life, at which point, my mother, who had been silent all this while in keeping with her policy of neutrality when her children clashed, sprang to my defense.

I heard her saying, "Now wait a minute, that's just not true," as I stormed out of the house. Finally.

I stood shaking and smoking beneath a tree until my mother came out to check up on me. She agreed that certain people inside had behaved badly but she wanted me to know that they had spoken out of concern for me. What really worried them was how heavy I had become.

Oh.

No one could remember ever seeing me so heavy and they were worried sick about my health.

Oh. From my perspective, Paul and his wife had been treating me like an obscenity in their household, an obscenity or a source of power that might spontaneously combust and engulf them in flames. How did I miss it? How could I not have felt all that caring and concern about my weight? Er—health.

I asked my mother: in the whole of my life had anyone in my family ever said anything about my size that had proved helpful? Effective? Kind?

I cannot recall one instance of being bullied or harassed about my size in school or by any of my peers. It had been all in the family.

Were they not aware that you couldn't shame people into changing their behavior? Didn't they know how heinous it was to add to the stigma and oppression already being experienced by a plus-sized person trapped in a culture with expectations so unrealistic that it airbrushes even its models?

When I got home from Essex that evening I felt so beat up, pummeled, and pounded on that I called six friends for assistance in normalizing my relations with both myself and the outside world. In the midst of all those phone calls, I experienced a searing moment of recognition that my cat was terminally ill.

After putting her down her 3 weeks later, I buried myself in finishing *The Odd Body Vanity Squad,* and when it was done, as per my agreement with my mother, I looked for and found a job.

When Alec suggested that acknowledging my obesity would mean acknowledging the trauma of abandonment, I balked. It would mean giving up the romance of the *Happy Hollisters* and *The Five Little Peppers*, the narrative in my own mind of a safe, supportive family circle and a charmed childhood. All those sweet, fun, picture-book memories were suddenly at risk. Had they not happened? But of course they had. My task now was to sort out the discrepancies between This Is What We Did and This Is How It Felt.

While sorting, I turned up a revealing memory of my mother from years ago. After she sold my grandparents' house on River Road, my brother Matt suffered what I considered to be a closely related nervous breakdown. My mother installed him in the psychiatric ward of a hospital in Pittsburgh and continued with her plans to leave for Russia the following week.

On the phone one night, she started speculating that maybe Matt wasn't just bipolar, maybe there was something else in his pathology, a touch of borderline this or paranoid that. In another round of our nature versus nurture debate, I reminded her of how my father had verbally abused Matt when the kid was 11, 12, 13.

When I started recalling brutal scenes of a chronically angry, chronically depressed man taking it out on his youngest son, my mother interrupted me with the words, "Stop it, stop!" I think she was crying. "Stop!" she said. "I *have* to believe that ours was a happy family!"

I was stunned. There it was. There it was on a personal level, a woman whose prime directive in life had revolved around doing one's duty wanting desperately to perceive herself as a success. And there it was, the opportunity for me to place her story inside another story, a larger one: the sanctification of home as the ultimate safe haven by a generation forged in the crucibles of a great depression and a global war.

Reinforced by flickering images on rapidly multiplying television sets, a dream had emerged of immaculate suburban households that identified woman as homemaker and man as breadwinner and moral compass, meticulous homes where the perfectly coiffed mother could be found basting a roast or icing a cake when the kids came home from school and the father wore a jacket and tie to the dinner table.

This black-and-white version of the self-contained household was not the first one or the only one to occur to humans. To be unconditionally included in one's tribe is a universal want, to know the peace and gladness of coming home.

How could I relinquish my dream of a snug and sheltering family? I had no other family. At the husband store, I had not read the policy on possible consequences, the fine print stating that if you left without a binding contract, hellfire would scorch your veins from Thanksgiving Eve to New Year's Day.

When my mother blurted her need to believe that ours had been a happy family, I felt sad and mad and guilty and depressed. And sorry for my mother. I wanted to say: We were a family, that's all. We are still a family and we are not finished.

If I had had the language at the time, I would have said: Mom. Let's turn the dichotomy between This Is What We Did and This Is How It Felt into a composite of This Is How It Was for Better and for Worse.

Mom, let us feel the pain.

Thou hast laid me in the lowest pit, in darkness, in the deeps.
PSALM 88:6

When I walked out of Dartmouth-Hitchcock on that January night, I knew that I was being forced out of myself, out into the cold. With two stents in my heart, I knew that for the near future, anxiety would be my scourge. And tears, too, for I had already wept plenty. I had not, however, anticipated the *pain*. It was waiting, a third layer beneath the panic and the tears.

I had experienced such pain before, but only in passing. I had smoked it away, swallowed it, and stuffed it down and stored it in fat. This time, I drilled to the bottom and said, "Right. Here it is. All the rage I sucked into my lungs. And the grief that I ate. For years."

The severity of it stunned me. Whatever it was that came up, it left me feeling annihilated but alive, like a still beating eviscerated heart. The pain of abandonment. The bloodcurdling absence of hope.

For the anxiety, there was Xanax. And there was visiting Phyllis, the mother of John from the old Windham days, a sweet and witty woman long since divorced, whose three children had settled elsewhere, and who had become my Brattleboro Mom. She was almost always home.

There was exercise 6 days a week, affirmations, deep breathing, and prayers in the morning and chamomile tea at night. There was church and tai chi. There were facials, massage, acupuncture, and cranial-sacral therapy administered by women whose wisdom, wackiness, and soothing ways proved as valuable as their expertise.

For the anxiety there was Michele to call any time of day or night, Alec to explain the mechanics and management of panic disorder, Jeff and Casey to promise that my heart was good for another 40 years, and Thomas and Jean to make the church my spiritual home.

For the pain, however, there was only one right thing: sit with it.

Only one thing to do: feel it. Sit and be present to myself, even if it meant feeling disconnected from all things, laid open to the darkness and chaos within.

The only way round was through it. There were no six tips or five steps, no goddess chakra bracelet, no detox diet or consciousness cleanse capable of making it go away. There were only the words of poets and philosophers, theologians, Buddhists, and psychologists about the redeeming and edifying power of pain.

For the poet Keats, pain was needed to attain mature personhood, to "school an intelligence and make it a soul." Pema Chodron encourages us to see our pain as a teaching; it will not dissolve or resolve, so we must make room for it and know that to be wholly alive and awake is to be repeatedly thrown out of the nest. The Persian poet Rumi wrote: "The wound is the place where the light enters in."

Occasionally I got an inkling that I was doing something right. After dinner and a movie with my best friend from the old Windham days, she remarked, "I can't believe how much you've changed. You used to have this thick, protective layer all around you. But now you're so clear and up front with your feelings."

And one day at Cardio-Rehab, Casey, ever astute and support-ive, observed in his snappy voice from across the room, "You don't have to wonder if you're on the right path, Martha, you never take a false step. Every time you lift up your foot, you set it down in exactly the right place."

For now, taking the next step meant sitting in the dark and reaching for the god-person inside the layered fat. I needed to find my truth inside the stores of adipose tissue, appease the longing for what might have been, turn inward, and there, find the joy and gladness of coming home.

FOUR

Until I was old enough and sufficiently well informed to engage in arguments with my father, we did not have a great deal to say to each other. On their wedding night, my father said to my mother, "I don't know anything about girls. You take care of the girls. I'll take care of the boys."

This could account for the lifelong state of unease that existed between us.

It was important to my father that I remain healthy and do well in school but I never sensed additional interest in the fact that I was taking ballet lessons or earning my Brownie Girl Scout Wings or swimming at the Y on Saturday mornings or spending most Sunday afternoons visiting the snakes in the reptile wing at the Staten Island Zoo.

I don't recall talking to him about whether I was adjusting and making new friends whenever he moved us to another town or which scientific principle I planned to demonstrate at the science fair or how I was going to choose between being an actress, an archeologist or a psychiatrist when I grew up. He could be familiar with my three brothers, but when it came to my sister and me, he seemed shy about knowing too much.

One day when I was 12, I flopped down on the living room floor with a notebook and pen to catch up on my diary. My father sat in his chair on the other side of the room reading the newspaper. He was always reading a newspaper. Once, when deliveries were delayed, he drove 50 miles through a blizzard to score a Sunday Times.

I enjoyed a close relationship with my diary. Although I dreamed of being different things when I grew up, I never dreamed of being a writer, for the simple fact that I was a writer. It was what I did. I wrote. I had just completed my first novel.

Something—what, exactly, I'll never know—compelled my father to look up from his newspaper and ask, "What are you doing?"

Since his eyes darted straight back to the paper, I am sure he didn't see my mouth drop open at this extraordinary display of interest in my life. I may have squirmed as I answered, "Writing in my diary."

"Are you keeping a diary?" he asked.

"Yes." I could not be sure whether this was a good thing or a bad thing, so I left it at that.

"That's great," he said.

"Why?"

"Because you never know, do you? The world could end tomorrow. But maybe centuries from now, maybe thousands of years into the future, when everything here is ashes and dust, beings from another planet will discover Earth and start digging things up. Their archeologists could dig up your diary and find out about life on Earth in the twentieth century. You could be making a real contribution to the scheme of things."

I believe he got up and wandered off at this point. I know he did not see the mix of fear, astonishment, and elation on my face. I had never heard my father imagine such a thing. He was a Harvard-educated, man-in-a-gray-flannel-suit type of guy, a public relations executive who read murder mysteries to relax and, to stay informed, 800-page tomes on history or current events.

He did not read science fiction, which might explain why he didn't ask by what miracle, fluke, or technological wonder the paper and ink of my diary would survive centuries or how these aliens would happen to understand English or why my loose-leaf notebooks would be the only account of the twentieth century to have withstood the nuclear or environmental holocaust that destroyed Earth. These things did not matter. It was the thought that mattered.

My father's vision opened up the universe for me. The possibility, although remote to the point of silly, that my diary might survive some immense stretch of time until beings from another planet turned up our remains, that my words might be found like an arrow head or a pharaoh's tomb and communicate something of value to another time and civilization felt oddly reassuring. It closed a loop somewhere. It brought me into the world and connected me to other times and places, no matter how distant, no matter how far. And so I continued to write.

Possibly, however, what impressed and pleased me most was the fact that my father had taken something I did seriously.

Years later, as my father lay dying, he prepared final requests for each one of his children. My mother called them our marching orders.

"Write," he told me. "Write seriously. Write novels."

I was amazed because my father and I had spent the past 20 years arguing over the fact that I was trying to be a writer instead of something sensible. As I sat with him during the last 4 hours of his super sensible life, he amazed me even more and broke my heart to pieces when he said, "Think of me from time to time."

As if I wouldn't.

There are many reasons for wanting to write. For me, high on the list, perhaps even higher than the chance of being discovered by aliens wielding hand brooms and trowels a hundred thousand years from now, is a desire to write for, and sometimes about, a difficult, complex, and vulnerable man who did not wish to be forgotten.

17
Call Me Pinocchio

ABOUT A YEAR AFTER MY HEART ATTACK, my brother
Paul was serving as composer-in-residence at the Institute for
Advanced Study in Princeton. He and his wife had rented a house
there and were extending invites for Easters, Thanksgivings, and
Christmases.

The guest list would always consist of some combination
of my mother, my brother Joe and his wife Gussie, one of their
two children, sometimes both, my buddy Gene and his girlfriend.
Brother Matt could never be there because he lived in Oman. And
sister Barney, living a reclusive life in western New York, had even
more reason than I to avoid our super successful brothers, as neither one of them had shown much use or affection for her in over
20 years.

Although I pined for a lavish holiday with my funny Porcellian
brothers, in Princeton no less, my old stamping ground, each invite saddled me with a dilemma. I don't know which aspect of the
dilemma was the more distressing: the deathly fear of traveling beyond my comfort zone either by car or by train; the hurt, humiliation, and fury I had not yet released from our Christmas in Essex 2
years previous; or the mortification of still being fat, the certainty
of feeling naked and raw beneath the glare of the self-appointed
and the self-righteous. I myself had not yet managed to evolve, and
with all their faults, love them still.

A friend suggested that I get a new hair color and do, buy a kick-ass dress, lay on the makeup, glitter, and feathers, hop into my car, and astonish them all by driving myself to New Jersey. I loved the idea of showing up unexpectedly at my brother's door with all my newfound audacity and aplomb. But it wasn't in me yet. Audacity and aplomb.

I did wonder what was the point of all this therapy, self-examination, and self-talk if I couldn't exhibit a whit of progress, if I couldn't face down just one phobia or somewhat raise my self-esteem. I only knew that I felt like a skulking beast. I did not wish to be seen, not by anyone in the outside world, especially the successful, legitimate, "healthy" members of my family.

It was not only shame or fear that kept me from going, but process as well. In order to heal and feel whole, I had to admit to having shared space with a family that still could not love, value, or validate me. Mental health resided in sacrificing the illusion of emotionally present people and staying away for now, even though it meant sitting home alone at Christmas with excruciating loneliness and loss.

During this time, the song "I'll Be Home for Christmas" made me ache every time I heard it. For two reasons. First, the overseas soldier who sings it may never make it home and second, at least *he* has a home to go home to.

There were other reasons for not joining the family in Princeton, one of them reason enough to cancel a drive across town to say nothing of an 8-hour train ride or road trip. I experienced my first colitis attack one night on my way to my first Toastmasters Meeting. I didn't know what it was; I had no idea what I was in for. I assumed it was a violent diarrhea and got through the meeting okay.

Ulcerative colitis is an inflammatory bowel disease that affects the colon and rectum in the most inconveniencing ways. Mine hit with confounding force. For a year and a half I frequently without warning lost control of my bowels. By some miracle I always managed to "let go" *after* leaving the office or the party or the gym, although I rarely made it to the toilet in time, sometimes just barely made it to the car, all of which left me with appalling messes to clean and symptoms like bleeding, exhaustion, and at one point, anemia (but not weight loss, worse luck).

I am grateful that I never lost control while at work or church or the movies or while standing in line at the post office, but the disgustingness of it made me a source of drastic embarrassment to myself. It was liquid shit and the unpredictable, quick loss of control felt stupefying. After an attack, whenever I could, I lay down and wondered *what the hell*. It seemed the ultimate in being alone. This was not something I could share.

It became my excuse for not being more ambitious about speech projects at Toastmasters, for limiting myself to the 2-minute Table Topics or Word of the Day. It became my excuse for not volunteering at church, not even for coffee hour, for not continuing my classes in American Sign Language, for not joining family at Christmas, and for not visiting when my Aunt Martha fell, broke her hip, and entered a rehabilitation facility from which she would never emerge.

Aunt Martha lingered for a year while my 86-year-old mother drove back and forth between Pittsburgh and Crofton, Maryland, to take charge of things, and with each stage of the dying process, to sell her younger sister's car, empty out her apartment, settle her affairs, notify friends, manage her estate, execute the terms of her will, decide which heirloom should go where, and plan two memorial services. The colitis prevented me from assisting my mother at this time and from dealing with the slow, wasting demise of a dear and doting aunt who had never married and had made our family her own.

My gastroenterologist insisted that my colitis had nothing to do with either my diet or my nerves, which infuriated me because it left me with no acceptable course of action. I told him it was high time he read *The Second Brain*. He rolled his eyes and told me to pick up a copy of *How Doctors Think*.

He did agree that prednisone (steroids!) was not the way to go and prescribed instead a hydrocortisone enema. With the best of intentions I picked up the paraphernalia at the Hotel Pharmacy.

But when I got home, I stashed the three white paper bags into a kitchen cupboard for some future time when I felt ready to deal with them. Which turned out to be never. I could not imagine causing any more aggravation to that part of my body.

My way of dealing was to go to a trendy boutique in town, pick out a bright pink tote bag with pockets and zippers, and equip it with towels and washcloths, diaper wipes and medicated cooling pads, underwear and extra pairs of pants and socks. I kept it in my car.

When I told Alec about this, he scolded me for spending money on a bag I did not need. I scolded him for missing the point. It was *pink*. I had chosen *pink* over gunmetal and beige. I had chosen whimsy and flash for my emergency kit to offset the indignity behind its use.

I determined to view the colitis as some sort of violent, outlandish detoxification. I was shitting my gut feelings out, releasing a lifetime of crap. I believed that if I just held on and continued processing my pain and my fears, I would grow out of the state of infancy I'd been reduced to and begin again, like new.

I often wondered about the baby Martha who had been left alone in the dark crying for hours. She must have soiled quite a few diapers while waiting for someone to come into the room and pick her up, clean and feed her. Was I connecting with her helplessness? Perhaps. Was this therapeutic? One could only hope.

Another inconvenience at this time was SVT benign tachycardia, which was how I ended up in the hospital in the first place. Three months after my stay at Dartmouth-Hitchcock, I went into rapid heartbeat again. I was so alarmed that I called Rescue. (The paramedics took one look at me and asked where I kept the Xanax.) The third, fourth, and fifth times it happened I tapped neighbors and work colleagues for rides to the ER. After that I simply drove myself to the hospital, oftentimes at two o'clock in the morning, to receive the only treatment that seemed to work for me, an IV shot of adenosine, a tricky drug that stops the heart and restarts it.

It got to the point where they just waved me in when they saw me coming and before I had even gotten horizontal on the gurney,

I'd have three people working on me, one hooking me up to the heart monitor, another sticking me with electrodes for an EKG, and a third poking holes in my arm to start an IV. Sometimes I found myself telling *them* what to do. You'll never find a vein in the arm, go for the hand. No, no, not esmolol, use adenosine. It works. No, not 6 units, but 12. Where's the doctor, you can't administer this drug without a doctor present.

It became another excuse for not going anywhere. Despite Jeff and Casey's assurances that every emergency room from here to Wherever and Back Again was equipped with adenosine and staff who knew how to use it, the thought of being on a train or highway, slipping into SVT, and having to go to a strange ER paralyzed me.

At Brattleboro Memorial, the folks were completely competent, calm, and good-humored. And every time I reported my latest episode to Jeff with my face long and my spirits sunk low, every time I asked, what's *wrong* with me, he would say, "Nothing. You're fine. It's just you. It's what you do." This was followed by a big fond, friendly smile that seemed to say: and what you are and what you do is wonderful. A little nutty, but wonderful.

Despite these reassurances, I lived in terror of these episodes. I was told repeatedly that mine was not a life-threatening condition and that my heart was healthy and still I greeted each event with dismay. For one thing, the rapid heart rate propelled me into a state of extreme physical discomfort and anxiety. Second, I harbored fears of something going horribly wrong during treatment: my heart would stop but not restart, a distracted nurse would flush the wrong drug into my veins, or an MRSA super bug would colonize my nostrils. Third, the drug itself produced the most horrendous sensation, something like being smothered with a pillow and tossed out of a 20-story window simultaneously.

I lived in terror of these episodes, and yet I refused the treatment that was 99 percent successful in eliminating the problem: ablation. Unfortunately, it resembled the cardiac catheterization, an invasive procedure that was still too fresh in my memory. According to Alec, I kept postponing the ablation because then I would have no excuse to go someplace where people were kind, where people would take care of me, run tests and pronounce me not dead but fully alive.

In retrospect, that may have been true. But at the time, I believed that, like the colitis, the tachycardia was a manifestation of an inner state of imbalance and that once my psychological stressors had been addressed, the episodes would become less frequent. It was all in my head and the mind can heal the body and the soul can heal itself. Salvation is built into our being.

The colitis did finally abate after a year and half, a welcome relief that coincided with a drop in the number and intensity of my anxiety attacks and a daily regimen of Omega 3 and probiotics. The debate over whether I should treat the SVT by going up to Dartmouth-Hitchcock for the ablation continues to this day.

I was always refusing treatment: no ablation for the SVT, no steroids or enema for the colitis, no gastric bypass, banding or sleeve gastrectomy for the obesity, and no antidepressants or buspirone for anxiety disorder. Why?

Whatever I was doing, I knew I had to do it myself. Whatever I was hoping to achieve, it had to be real and hard won. Yes, it felt like death at times. It had to. I had to keep reminding myself that *I* was not dying. Something inside of me was. My best medicine was pain, grief, tears.

One day I met my match, however, a symptom that could not be ignored or a treatment postponed. I had gone into SVT and after trying all the techniques I'd been taught to convert it, reported to the ER. The dread drug adenosine had been administered. I felt fine and was just waiting for the results of my blood work to come back from the lab.

After what seemed an unusually long wait, the doctor on duty entered and announced with a dour face that my blood test had been normal. Everything good. Except for one thing. Something they hadn't even been looking for. My blood sugar level was reading 533. (A healthy number would be no higher than 99 after fasting while 2 hours after eating, it should be no more than 140.)

The attending physician said it would be irresponsible for him to let me go until the issue had been addressed. They had called my doctor. They had called my diabetes educator. They were all discussing a course of action that might include keeping me overnight. I was stunned.

I had been outwitting my diabetes for 10 years. I had kept it in check with diet and exercise and I'd been doing it so well that I wasn't even testing my blood sugar on a daily or regular basis. For 10 years I had been telling myself, I don't *really* have diabetes. When people asked, I would say, I *sort of* have diabetes.

Hoty, my smart and chipper diabetes educator, showed up at the ER with a taut, grim face. He said, "Guess what, my dear, you're going on drugs. Today. The nurse is coming in to give you insulin to bring your blood sugar down before we decide whether we're going to let you out of here, and we're calling in a prescription to your pharmacy for metformin. So guess what, my dear, you don't have a choice."

As it turned out, I had such a bad reaction to the metformin that a week later Hoty was showing me how to inject myself with insulin. (Which is considered by many to be the lesser of two evils.) Within minutes of arriving home from learning how to inject myself, my mind had spun out half a dozen nightmare scenarios involving the flex pens I would be using, which in actual fact make injections mercifully easy. I envisioned myself getting a tainted pen with something quick and deadly in it, or an empty pen liable to deliver a lethal air bubble into my veins, or a mechanically faulty pen that would slip and go haywire while I was pushing the plunger and rush a fatally high dose of insulin into my body.

On a more practical level, I wondered how injecting myself twice every morning and once before each meal was going to fit into the rest of my life. For instance, dining out. To prevent an abrupt drop in blood sugar, it was necessary to eat 10 minutes after taking the Novolog[R]. (What if I *didn't* eat 10 minutes after? Would I *die*?) I feared feeling like a real klutz in restaurants, excusing myself and leaving the table for cramped, dimly lit bathroom stalls to stick a needle in my gut. Was I doomed? Was I to be forever encumbered with the paraphernalia that goes with a glucose meter and injections, charged with the task of packing, storing, and properly disposing of lancets, bloody test strips, needles, alcohol swabs, and insulin delivery systems? Was I damned? Getting older, getting fatter, jabbing myself with needles to stave off the apparently inevitable complications of this "devastating" and "life-threatening" disease? Was this me? No.

W. H. Auden wrote that we would rather die in our dread than let our illusions die, we would rather be ruined than changed. I was determined not to be ruined. I wanted Life.

The real problem with injecting myself would be trying to beat the diabetes by losing weight when the chief side effect of taking insulin was weight gain.

One day, while seated in the waiting room at the Brattleboro Pastoral Counseling Center, I flashed on to an image of Pinocchio. It came out of nowhere. First, I *saw* Pinocchio. Then I *felt* Pinocchio. And then I *was* Pinocchio, as though his image had been projected onto my body and quickly absorbed. A wooden puppet waiting to be converted into a real boy. Flesh and blood.

Alec was delighted to hear it, not because I identified with Pinocchio necessarily but because for the first time ever, I had come in, sat down and told him how I felt. I had not described a feeling and then asked, "Is that okay, is that all right, does it make sense?" This was a significant shift for me, a sign of improved mental health.

I had a theory as to how I happened to be made of wood. My fear of death came early and without pity. I was so unaccepting of death, I think I made a pact with myself and/or God (whoever *he* was) based on an incredibly flawed proposition: if I am not human, I am not mortal; if I am not mortal, I cannot die.

It could not have been a conscious decision. It could only have been subliminal, the need and the effort to believe that somehow I was not human. I was different, aloof, independent, alone. I was gifted. I was fat. A writer, an *artiste,* smarter than anyone and too fat to participate. No way was I human. *They die.*

Maybe it was why I never married, never had children. That

was something humans did, and other animals, but not me. If I held myself in abeyance, if I lived in my head, I would not be subject to disappointment, death, and decay.

By the time I reached midlife, I had settled on obesity as my primary means of exempting myself from the human race. With aging not only was I not human, I was *sub* human, society's nightmare: a woman over 40, overweight, postmenopausal, single, childless, in short, a freak.

No wonder I wasn't losing weight. If I lost weight, I might attract a man and be pinned down. If I lost weight, I might take myself seriously as a responsible human being and start contributing to my community. I might even travel, I might go out into the world and get killed. If I lost weight, I risked conversion from wood to flesh, *I might get healthy and die!*

No wonder I was shitting my guts out and racing my heart. I had begun to challenge basic concepts about my way of being in the world. By moving closer toward life, I was inviting death in. Naturally I was terrified 85 percent of the time.

In the midst of this, over a 6-month stretch, I was beset by a series of infelicitous events.

A certifiable paranoid schizophrenic with a history of harassing her neighbors moved into the studio apartment below me. She banged on her ceiling whenever she heard me upstairs in my kitchen, pounded on her walls in the pre-dawn hours, and shouted obscenities at me as I walked to my car in the morning. I phoned the folks at the Health Care and Rehabilitation Services every other day to insist that they find other accommodations for her. It took them 3 months, but they did.

At this same time I experienced a sudden visitation of mice. They were bold, they were everywhere, wriggling up out of the toaster and through the stovetop burners, leaping in and out of the garbage pail, carrying out what looked like reconnaissance missions on top of my dresser while I sat reading in bed, knocking spice jars off the shelves in the middle of the night. I tried thinking of them as amusing little companions or the price one pays for living in the country, but after all my humane efforts to be rid of them failed and after I found evidence that they were gnawing food particles out of wet sponges left in the sink, I asked my landlord to take care of them. He did.

I found a lump in my breast, which kicked off a morbid month of waiting, wondering, and fearing the worst. It turned out to be nothing. I hit and killed a cat with my car. At the gym, a man dropped dead on the treadmill next to mine. I got a violent flu for the first and only time in my life. During a winter storm, half a tree fell on my parked car and smashed the windshield and hood. I came down with a fever of 103°F for no apparent reason. The tension at work between a colleague and me was tying me up in knots.

One day in therapy, as I tallied and lamented this cloudburst of life's predicaments, Alec stopped me, grinned and exclaimed, "Welcome to the human race."

It all felt terrible, but it seemed *good*.

And even when it didn't feel good, it at least felt better. Anxiety ceased to be the main event every day. It hogged every other day and then every third day, and so forth and so on. Sometimes it lifted for a whole week, then returned with a vengeance to consume another month before backing off to every other day again and then every other week.

At times when I looked outside myself, I experienced surprising clarity and when I looked inside, there was new calm. After 3 years I began to believe, without Alec or Jeff or Casey or Thomas or Michele telling me so, that I would emerge from this wind tunnel.

But I had no idea who I would be when I did. It was frightening, not in the way of anxiety, but in the uncertain, unpredictable way of real life. I couldn't even say that when I came out of the tunnel I would still be a writer.

I had not written anything since the heart attack. As for my diary, which had been my ally from age 11, I hadn't kept it up. Instead of a narrative, I had accumulated a hodgepodge of letters and emails, newspaper articles, and wild thoughts scribbled during panic attacks, usually in the middle of the night. Even after 3 years, I was finding it impossible to sit down with just me in the room, impossible to give shape to what I was feeling inside, impossible to write without a lit cigarette in my hand.

There were other reasons for not maintaining my diary. The grind of trying to feel safe and stay calm, the adrenaline rushes, the colitis, and the daily workouts along with stress and pressure at the office, were wearing me out. My life felt gray, my prospects nil. I wasn't keeping up with my diary because I had lost interest in myself. I had lost interest in my own story.

I don't know which frightened me more, the fact that I had lost interest in my own story or the possibility that I had ceased being a writer. Writing had been a vital defense against death. Being a writer had been the healthiest of my alternatives to being human.

It was time to just plunge. I dedicated my 2-week summer vacation to revising Book One of *The Secret Name of God*.

It would be a beginning. But I needed a safe place in which to do it. Not my own home, not yet. I might start smoking again. I asked my Brattleboro Mom Phyllis if we could set up a table on her front lawn underneath the apple tree.

For 2 weeks, while she sat reading in her Adirondack chair or puttered in and out of her apartment making tea and light meals, I sat and wrote. The weather held out, the summer breezes felt fine, while I chewed on cinnamon-flavored Tea Tree Australian Chewing Sticks and forced myself back into the writing mode, which means sitting with oneself only, whether barren or overflowing, feeling too little or too much, for long periods of time. It was painful, slow and dull.

Gradually over that summer, I remembered how to sit silent and alone at my desk.

Yes, things were getting better. And yet Alec kept reminding me that things would never be best. Just as I needed to give up the dream of a magical childhood, there was another magical time that had to be discarded. The perfect future I had in mind. The future where, by achieving my most cherished goals, I would obliterate all fear, anxiety, anger, and shame. It was the future where I would never again feel abandoned or alone.

Alec liked saying, "Good luck with that."

Such feelings would always be with me, he said. The trick was to feel them and know that I was still okay. He used the word okay, I preferred safe.

Code words for lovable.

And loved.

18
Mad Genius Bohemians

I N HIGH SCHOOL, my best friend Barbara and I lived in a
world of dreams and extremes, a world of our own making.
She was an artist, I a writer. We were brilliant, indestructible, and
wild.

Although we had a high regard for all great art and literature,
we steeped ourselves in the life stories of the passionate, reckless,
sometimes genuinely insane, writers, poets, and painters, musicians and performers of the nineteenth-century and first three decades of the twentieth. We honored them and set fire to our own
existence by living in a near continual state of ecstatic creativity
and abandon.

A thing wasn't just funny, it was hilarious and liable to send
us into hysterics; a thing wasn't just sad, it was either unbearably
poignant or operatic; we were never just happy, we were euphoric,
exalted, or so overjoyed we could cry.

We called ourselves mad genius bohemians.

The distinguishing characteristic of mad genius bohemians is
that they have a passion, something they believe or actively engage
in that makes their spirits soar. And their best feature is their joie
de vivre.

In musical theatre, characters invariably reach a moment when they can no longer contain the swell of feelings within and so must spontaneously burst into song. The mad genius bohemian is familiar with that moment and inclined to turn the impulse to sing into an exuberant, spiritually sourced state of being.

Mad genius bohemians are loving and creative, filled with wonder, at heart a bit uncivilized. They are wise to the world but it is not in their nature to be cynical. They would rather stay hungry and foolish than turn bitter and mean.

Although my salad days as a mad genius bohemian seemed long gone, Alec once noted, "There is something innate in you that drives you continually toward creation."

I was 12 when I first heard the "Carousel Waltz" from the Rodgers and Hammerstein musical *Carousel*. I distinctly remember weeping and swaying to this jaunty, buoyant overture and thinking, this is *it*, this is want I want to do! I want to create and reveal to others this same pure joy!

In that moment I pledged myself, I took vows in what felt like a righteous, rapturous pact with God.

Once I started writing with purpose, I found ingenious ways to play hooky from school. Sometimes I asked my mother outright if I might stay home so I could work on my latest novel. She was startled or impressed enough to occasionally say yes and years later my father attributed all my failings in life to this leniency. I feel only gratitude. She was my first reader.

In high school, after finishing our homework, under cover of night, Barbara and I changed into mad genius bohemians. Making full use of the Princeton University campus as our all-hours adventure park, crash pad, and cabaret, between bouts of roaming, singing, and laughing hysterically, we created. She drafted paintings and graphic novels, I scribbled out novels, screenplays, short stories, and poems.

Despite my vow to communicate the joy found in the "Carousel Waltz," my stories were not happy ones. Joy was not just merriment. Joy had layers and depth. My novels usually involved a handsome but haunted hero who dies young. One book, inspired by my mad crush on a classmate studying to be a concert pianist, concluded with a brilliant nineteenth-century pianist deliberately burning his hands.

After seeing a performance of Benjamin Britten's *Noye's Fludde,* I wrote what I called a modern medieval musical miracle play, which featured Death itself as a comely young man who seeks shelter one night in a monastic school where he engages the abbot in a debate over man's fate and makes his final point by leading all the students away at sunrise, singing, beautifully, of course, in an epidemic of plague.

I was never far from a theatre. I acted quite a bit and received high praise for my performance as Gertrude in *Hamlet.* I took piano lessons for a number of years and composed interesting music for the accordion. I dabbled in modern dance. For a final project in gym class, I choreographed and performed an interpretation of the first movement of Carl Orff's *Carmina Burana.*

Some of my more ambitious projects, which did not reach completion, were an 8 mm film about young women feeling strangely, atavistically drawn to a tall, carved pillar in the forest, a musical adaptation of *Wuthering Heights* and a screenplay for the John Knowles novel *A Separate Peace.*

After high school, it was unpublished novels and then the musicals—produced, revised, dropped—then back to unpublished novels again. It took me 24 years and three different colleges to complete a B.A. degree. For paying the bills, it was bars and restaurants, then administrative work in academic and nonprofit environments.

After a certain age, there was so much wrong with this picture that despite my lively interests, pursuits, and social life, I carried within me a low-grade depression which I persistently self-medicated with food.

I should have been a leading light on Broadway or a successfully published author or both, at any rate, influential and financially sound.

Or I should have made a successful marriage with a successful man and together we should have made six children. I would have wanted a large family. By now, my house should have been filling up with the children of my children.

Or I should have finished college when I was supposed to. I should have been a journalist or an editor at a big publishing house or a beloved ivy-league professor.

After losing my job at SIT at the unemployable age of 52, when not looking for work, I concentrated on rewriting *The Secret Name of God* for the thirty-ninth time, writing *The Odd Body Vanity Squad* and developing detailed proposals for six more books, one of which would incorporate a sweeping revision of the five musicals.

Desperate for work, I was applying for jobs at Walmart and Dunkin' Donuts when I found a position as a sort-of all-round office person for 10 hours a week coordinating statewide trainings at a nonprofit health education organization in town.

Johanna, my new boss, was a petite, well-groomed, super-fit, super-driven woman who had a capacity and a reputation for making any colleague standing within 3 feet of her batshit crazy. At the time of my hire, it was just the two of us, plus a part-time bookkeeper who eventually quit to protect her blood pressure from the kind of havoc Johanna could create.

When I arrived, the organization was on the verge of implosion owing to Johanna's loss of focus and a high turnover rate for the position I had just filled. My 10 hours a week turned almost at once into 30 and then 40, as together we reassembled the organization, caught up on projects and deadlines that should have been completed 5 months previous, and got things moving again. We worked well together. She was appreciative, supportive, incredibly generous, and frequently out of town for trainings, meetings, and conferences.

Despite the trials of working for an overextended, overstressed executive director, I felt stimulated by the administrative challenges of rebooting an organization and then growing it, excited by the mission of the organization, genuinely fond of Johanna, and enthusiastic about what I was absorbing from her professional manner, integrity, and skills.

Nonetheless, at the time of my heart attack, I was pretty much what my brother Joe had envisioned for me, an office manager. And don't think it didn't gall me. Or hurt. With only myself to blame. Because novel-writing (not journalism, not even freelancing) was the only career I had ever wanted, I had failed to carve out some other career commensurate with my talents and potential.

At almost 60, however, it seemed advisable to try making careers out of my day jobs because if the writing thing never panned out, I could end life as one of the mentally ill homeless filling up shopping carts with returnable soda cans. I had spent 10 years at Smith and SIT dithering between advancing myself in a professional capacity or staying on track with my writing until I reached my mid-fifties without having achieved distinction in either direction. The punishment would be bag-ladydom, for sure.

Inspired by the coincidence of my wake-up call and my apprenticeship under Johanna, I began perusing suitable job descriptions. Senior Writer. Content Writer. Director Editorial Services. Publications Managing Editor. Web and Social Media Writer. Development Communications. Online Marketing Manager.

There was no doubt in my mind that if I applied all of my time, energy, and nerve, I could have done these jobs and done them well, even if it meant going back to school, and I gave these matters considerable thought. It was one thing to be almost 30 or 40 and fear ending up as a bag lady and quite another to be almost 60. At 60, when there is less time, energy, and opportunity for securing the means to avoid it, the specter of dumpster diving and sleeping in doorways looms large.

My horizon opened up when our organization was awarded a $1.5 million federal grant to oversee the launch of a statewide public awareness and training campaign for youth suicide prevention in Vermont. We knocked down walls to double the size of our office, invested in new technology, office equipment and furniture, and bulked up to a five-and-a-half-person staff while keeping track of an increased number of trainers, consultants, partners, coalitions, and state agencies.

When we hired a professional marketing firm in Burlington to create our campaign and materials, I assumed the role of coordinating the many marketing pieces and some of the development. In addition to my manifold administrative duties at work, I read up on youth suicide prevention and compiled a huge file of research materials. I then wrote all the copy and helped in the design for posters, brochures, wallet cards, e-newsletters, training calendars, flyers, banners, and floor displays, press releases, public announcements and bulk mailings. I also wrote the suicide prevention handbook for use in our trainings and the content for two new websites.

I took tremendous satisfaction in this. I enjoyed collaborating with our new project manager, Brian, especially during our "banana breaks," when we ate our mid-morning snack while working out the campaign's voice, approach, and core message. We favored the emerging fields of resilience and positive psychology.

But there was trouble ahead. Johanna alternated between encouraging me to pursue marketing and communications and holding me back—I never knew who was going to show up for work that day—and she failed to head off a competitive relationship between a colleague and myself that led to harrowing tension in the workplace, destructive office politics, and the resignation of . . . not me.

There was something else—my own awareness that I may have been doing good work but that in the sphere of professional appearance, dress, and demeanor, when weighed, I could be found seriously wanting. To begin with, my 300 pounds did not bode well for an organization that promoted public health and health education, especially one that was stepping into a larger, federally funded arena.

And there was my wardrobe. I was not dressing to enhance my appearance. (No appearance to enhance.) Since I expected to lose a hundred pounds any minute, I saw no point in spending real money on decent clothes. At this point in my life, I ordered from plus-sized catalogues and dressed the same for the gym, the movies, the workplace, and home in sneakers, baggy pants, and stained tee-shirts worn underneath unbuttoned big shirts, unless it was hot, and then it was just the stained tees. At home I tended to wear not much of anything because I found clothes so stifling.

Most of our business was conducted off site, so my position did not bring me into contact with our clients or public. I worked behind the scenes, but even there I apparently began to fall short, which I discovered when I came upon a note Johanna had written expressing concern that my raspy, sporadically disappearing voice was no longer suitable for answering the phone.

It wasn't just dress, it was demeanor: conduct, body language, tone of voice, facial expressions. What I considered challenging behavior on my part for the sake of brainstorming or vigorous problem solving, Johanna perceived as argumentative and disrespectful.

What had begun as a mutually admiring and productive work relationship was deteriorating into a tug-of-war that exacerbated my fat shame. Johanna was a loving, nurturing soul, and she would have been appalled if she knew I suspected her of fat prejudice, but it just seemed to emanate from her, perhaps without her even knowing. In her presence I felt the same mortification my mother could still generate in me. It is in our culture, our conscience, our mental processes.

It was in Johanna's voice, in her quietly dismayed, quietly horrified looks from across the room. It was in her puzzlement one day when she saw that my mother was small, fit, and well dressed, and another day in her incredulity when she asked, *"You read Bon Appétit?"* She admitted once that she almost didn't hire me because of concerns about my weight. Er—health. I believe that in the end it interfered with her ability to correctly evaluate my performance and invest in my true potential.

My workdays concluded in ever-greater states of high dudgeon because I knew I could do more if Johanna would let me— or could I?

My phobias limited me as much as my wardrobe. I missed conferences in Orlando, Washington, and Santa Fe because I would not fly. I missed trainings and meetings in places as easy to get to as Montpelier and Burlington. I panicked at the thought of driving to places I had never been before, encountering high-speed traffic on highways with more than two lanes, getting lost, driving through a thunderstorm, or finding myself among only strangers.

All these things stood between me and those glamorous communications and web content jobs I wanted to do—or did I?

By now, I was developing a real distaste for the artificiality of workplace protocol. I began to long for restaurants again, where people threw knives at each other and had done with it. I remember that 15 years earlier, I couldn't wait to get out of the restaurant business because the hours had placed me on the fringe of society by stealing my nights, weekends, and holidays. But now the nine-to-five grind was pulping my soul. Did I really want to devote the rest of my time on earth to cultivating my professional appearance, soft skills, and office etiquette?

Life was short and getting shorter. I was not writing. I was coming home exhausted, depressed, discouraged, and shamed. I watched *Jeopardy!* while eating a very good dinner and then flopped in front of a movie while taking the chocolate cure that was still meant to compensate for my lack of companionship, sex, or plans, purposefulness or God.

And the years were passing. The ghost voices were telling me, not for the first time, to give up my dream. And why not? I was closing in on my sixties, and I feared I had nothing, nothing, to show for it.

Except for the stories I had written. And the ones I still wanted to write.

Deep down inside of me, in a remembered, radiant abyss, the mad genius bohemian yet lived.

Three years out of the hospital, my anxiety attacks eased up. They could still be potent but they were fewer and farther between. I understood them now. Anxiety diverted me from feelings that my inner child considered dangerous. What's this, a feeling? Oh no, let this pain in my chest shout heart attack, so I can focus on that instead! When I asked Alec why I would choose the prospect of sudden death, which was the worst thing I could imagine, over feeling abandoned, he said, "Because it's familiar."

After 3 hectic, myopic years, I could make out shapes in the space up ahead, although I still had no clear idea of who would be standing in the shower of light at the end of the tunnel.

I could go back to school and get a degree in marketing and communications.

Or I could join the increasing number of coaches who were leaving successful careers to follow their hearts and pursue their soul's mission, which was to go out and help others leave their careers, follow their hearts, and pursue their soul's mission.

Or I could go down to the husband store and pick out a distinguished, charming Princeton professor with a lucrative retirement plan, a Pulitzer Prize, and a head full of hair. Ancient Mediterranean civilizations make for good pillow talk. Or maybe Arthurian literature of the Middle Ages. If he could manage to look and sound like Ronald Colman, that would be just fine.

Or I could surrender to mad genius bohemianism and heed the words of Ayn Rand: "Do not let your fire go out, spark by irreplaceable spark, in the hopeless swamps of the approximate, the not-quite, the not-yet, the not-at-all. Do not let the hero in your soul perish, in lonely frustration for the life you deserve, but have never been able to reach. Check the road and the nature of your battle. The world you desire can be won. It exists, it is real, it is possible, it is yours."

At work one day, while gazing out the window at our scenic view of the Connecticut River, I was feeling so oppressed I had to remind myself that the choice had been mine every step of the way to work jobs that did not fully involve or engage me because they left mental space and time in my life for the only thing I wanted to do—write. Still, I was feeling smothered that day, taut and pinched, like a lobster cramping inside the shell he is outgrowing.

So I made a list. Not a list of things to do but of things to acquire. First and foremost, I needed a MacBook Pro. At home I was still using a 12-year-old Dell computer with an agonizingly slow dial-up system. Once while visiting, Michele tried logging onto Facebook and gave up after 45 minutes.

As a result, I never went online. But serious writers had to be online. For a number of reasons, including incredible shrinking publishing houses, exploding social media, and attractive self-publishing options, it was becoming compulsory for authors to establish platforms and take on the cost, stress, and pains of marketing their work and promoting themselves.

My life away from the workplace thus far had been gadgetless. I was the only person I knew who didn't own a cell phone. So second on my list after a MacBook Pro was an iPhone to go with it. I would probably need a Kindle and just for the hell of it, I threw in an iPod. If the iPad had been around at the time, I would have wanted that, too.

I needed to create an author website and a blog. I needed to be released from this job that was destroying my morale. I needed freedom from having to work at all, freedom to write full time. I needed my health back. I had to lose weight. I needed an agent, a book contract, and publisher.

I understood that it was unlikely for a no-name novelist to get published or for a published novelist to make a living as such. But if I gave up after all these years, I would have to wonder what my whole life had been about. I had set my course a long time ago and the only thing that made sense now would be to follow through on it, regardless of where it might lead.

Within 2 months, my first wish was granted. My mother agreed to send money for a MacBook Pro. My sweet lovely Aunt Martha had died and the money came out of her estate.

I was so awed by my sleek new laptop that it actually frightened me and sat on my desk at home for 3 months, peeked at and skirted like a charming but cunning animal. One day I decided to stop being silly. Tingling and trembling, I sat myself down and launched into cyberspace, where I encountered almost at once my point of no return.

> *The call to adventure is the point in a person's life when they are first given notice that everything is going to change, whether they know it or not.*
>
> —Joseph Campbell

19
The Hound of Heaven

IN THE LONG TALKS OF MY YOUTH, particularly in conversations with my brother Paul or my buddy John at Windham,
when the topic turned to the nature of the universe, I invariably argued for the Absolute. There had to be a universal absolute. There
could be no safety and no sense in a universe without a capital G
God.

He didn't have to be listening or making covenants with us. But
there had to be a shadow universe, a totality outside of energy and
matter permeated by something relevant to our experience, something we could participate in and count on as everlasting.

There could be no joy in a world that did not feel safe or make
sense, which meant that my life had hinged on a desire to feel
secure in a universe that continually and constitutionally argued
against it. Result, anxiety. If the one constant of life was to be in
flux, and I wanted to be stable, then I had to step outside of life. I
did. Result, it was cold out there. I warmed myself with food.

The strategy had emerged early on: to be not vulnerable,
therefore not actually present, therefore not human and mortal,
therefore not subject to death. Result, an outcome the opposite of
what was intended. To be always hurting and in need of numbing
the hurt.

Alec described me one day as the crying baby who wants to

be picked up. Jung observed that something in each of us wishes to remain a child, conscious only of the ego, and that our preference is for a comfortable life. He noted that the safe life, however, discourages growth. It limits the opportunity to develop a larger, more vibrant consciousness.

In that vein, others maintain that our attachment to stability, certainty, and permanence is irrational. Crazy making. The only sane response to life is to be at peace with ambiguity. Breathe, breathe, lean into the moment and embrace the godlessness and groundlessness of our existence. Let go.

Or compromise. Assume that God inhabits a reality outside our consciousness and ability to comprehend. If God is the thing we cannot conceive of at the edge of the universe, the "space" that space is filling, the infinitude we cannot quite grasp, then he as He also cannot be conceived of. Or addressed. This God may be there, but the moment he is defined, He is gone.

As I approached my sixtieth birthday, all I knew for sure was that for me spirituality resided in religion and that religion was fellowship and that the Episcopal Church would sustain me while I wandered at my leisure through the cold storage between the God of certainty and the no-God of no-certainty.

Thomas and our Priest Associate Jean wandered with me at this time. I did not go to them as an agnostic. I went one day as an atheist and another day as a believer. I despised God because he was impossible to prove. I despised him because his non-existence was more believable than his existence. I had to *know*. I had to be as certain of his presence in the universe as I could be of the laws governing all properties and events within it and throughout the whole of it. If I could not know for certain that God existed, I could not be bothered with him.

After years of debate, Thomas begged me to stop thinking. "Just believe, Martha, please? Don't think about it, don't worry about it, please? It doesn't matter if it's true or not, just try it. Try believing. Try it for a month and see what happens."

I tried it and then started spending more time with Jean. Jean was in her late seventies, born in the Midwest, raised in New

England. Her father had been a Congregational minister who deserted his family for a woman he met during the war. Jean went on to date only seminarians. She wanted to be a minister, but because that was not an option at the time, she thought the next best thing would be to marry one.

So she did. She had four children and slid into a bout of alcoholism that helped destroy the marriage. One day a therapist suggested that she just get on with things and become a priest, which was now possible. She went to Episcopal Divinity School and at age 56, was ordained to be what she always felt she should have been.

"I'm not ready to die," I said to her one day. I was complaining about death again. "There's so much more I want to do."

Jean said, "Me, too."

I gave her a puzzled look. "No, but really, I have *so much* I still want to accomplish."

She replied, "So have I."

I fell silent for a moment. She didn't understand. She couldn't. Jean was 20 years older than I, she had had her life: husband, home, children, holidays not alone, recovery and a rewarding career. She was almost 80, for Chrissake.

I persisted. "But I feel like I haven't even *begun* to do all the things I planned on doing."

With knowing eyes, Jean laughed in her genuinely good-humored way. "Me, too! I'm not finished, not by any means!"

Whether intentionally or not, Jean reminded me that those of us fortunate enough to reach the natural end of our lives may conclude there is something more important than what we have done or left undone, what we did or did not do. If we are very fortunate, we will believe we are not finished no matter how long we live, because there is always something worth doing.

This sense that we may never be done makes the *doing* part of our lives almost incidental. There needs to be something more to the point than checking off items on a bucket list, something more wonderful and perfect, something other and beyond.

One day Jean introduced me to "The Hound of Heaven." It is a 182-line poem written by the English poet Francis Thompson, a scholar and a gentleman who spent much of his adult life homeless on the streets of London, depressed, suicidal, and addicted to laudanum. "The Hound of Heaven" first appeared in 1893 and gained traction as one of the great Catholic poems of all time.

It describes the flight of a headstrong, errant soul and the unhurried but unceasing pursuit of him by a loving God in the guise of a hound.

> I FLED Him, down the nights and down the days;
> I fled Him, down the arches of the years;
> I fled Him, down the labyrinthine ways
> Of my own mind; and in the mist of tears
> I hid from Him, and under running laughter.
> Up vistaed hopes I sped;
> And shot, precipitated,
> Adown Titanic glooms of chasmèd fears,
> From those strong Feet that followed, followed after.
> But with unhurrying chase,
> And unperturbèd pace,
> Deliberate speed, majestic instancy,
> They beat—and a Voice beat
> More instant than the Feet—
> "All things betray thee, who betrayest Me."

The Hound is an emissary of a Heaven that sends for us. Perhaps Jean wanted me to use the image of being unhurryingly but relentlessly pursued to address the fact that even though I couldn't believe, I still wanted to believe and that in my want there was something that just wasn't going to leave me alone.

After 11 years as our rector, Thomas moved on to a parish outside Boston and then Jean retired. I continued going to church but it would be a long time before I went back to the business of arguing with priests.

Maybe for a while I just needed to sit with mystery.

And maybe this felt possible because life was becoming reasonable again. Change had taken place not overnight, but in pieces, on its own terms. It was two steps back, three steps forward, one step back, a great leap forward and then a lapse, two leaps, a lull, and then another lapse, leap, lapse, plateau.

I had regained what I considered one of my most precious gifts: the ability to be alone. I was writing again. I still craved a cigarette every minute of every day and never so badly as when I was writing. But I stayed quit, frequently popping up from my chair to walk around in circles and thrashing my hands at the air until the brain-jitters passed.

I had learned to manage my anxiety attacks well enough so that I no longer lived in abject terror of them. Three years after my heart attack, with spring came modest signs that I was emerging from crisis mode and gathering momentum toward new life.

Michele had moved back to town and I was feeling much less alone in the world. I had hosted a welcome home party and out of the guests a new gang emerged, an old gang really. We had all known each other at SIT. We made sure we got together on a regular basis for potluck dinners, and we kept up with each other's stories in between times. I began to feel the substructure of a new support system, one that I had come by honestly, consisting of friends independent of a church congregation, who, like family, have to take you in, along with the paid professionals in my life.

In June I traveled to Beaver, Pennsylvania, for my Aunt Martha's graveside memorial service, a jaunt for some but a trek for agoraphobic me. My nephew Gene did the driving. It was a quick trip, first to Ithaca, where we helped Gene's girlfriend put up a commissioned piece of installation art in the Downtown Ithaca Commons, then to western New York to pick up my sister Barney, then south to Beaver, where we spent a memorable evening with a fair number of cousins, aunts, and uncles on Aunt Margie's porch.

I got through the entire trip without suffering a twinge of anxiety. This was a remarkable feat for which I had no explanation, although it helped that there were no thunderstorms or tornado watches, no episodes of SVT tachycardia, no recurrence of colitis, no fiery head-on collision, no lunatics lying in wait with guns, no strangers with evil intent. The outside world felt safe, bright, sunny, and refreshing. As we committed Aunt Martha's ashes to the Beaver Cemetery, I read a eulogy I had written. My grainy, husky, vanishing voice sounded strong and clear.

Back home, as soon as I stopped feeling intimidated by my new MacBook Pro and the exposure of venturing onto Facebook, I heard from Barbara, of all people, my best friend from high school and fellow mad genius bohemian. We had not made contact for 40 years. Through a series of lengthy, exuberant emails, I found myself reuniting with that younger, wilder part of myself.

I heard from other high school friends. And at the end of that summer I attended an elaborately orchestrated reunion in Putney of the old Windham theatre gang. Most of the key figures from my college days were there and the whole weekend, despite my nerves beforehand, felt deeply satisfying and sweet.

The angel in my whirlwind, if such a thing existed, was still nudging me, but outward now instead of inward, outward into the path of family, old friends, old, old friends and still older friends, forcing me to retrieve inner selves that had burrowed out of sight. I went along with what may have been Somebody's plan for me, feeling skittish but expectant and hungry for change. Something seemed to be brewing.

By the beginning of the fall, I knew what it was.

Another birthday had gone by, which added another year's worth of kick to the fear that I was wasting precious time trying to be something I was not, the smart-and-savvy-career-woman as modeled by my boss. Nine-to-five office work was not the life for a mad genius bohemian.

The catalyst appeared when Johanna created a new position and hired an operations manager who would rank above me. It created a situation that felt spookily similar to the circumstances attending my departure from SIT, where the arrival of a new dean had changed my status overnight from an indispensable administrator who had helped create the current infrastructure to the odd man out in what was to become the new scheme of things.

I could not, however, just quit. For women my age in the Brattleboro area, opportunities had withered. I faced age discrimination and probably weight discrimination as well. I had to wait to be fired so as to be eligible for unemployment insurance.

Every morning without fail I reported to an unpredictable, increasingly hostile work environment, where the rules were changed without notice and enforced without grace; where my status, roles, and responsibilities seemed to inscrutably shift, reverse, and shift again. One day things felt fine—I was treated like part of the team and slated for training in new multimedia programs—and the next day I was batted about like a child, a nuisance, and most insulting of all, an outsider.

It was dizzyingly, nauseatingly stressful but I was able to hold on because my feelings were clear. For the first time in my life I felt confident that *I* was not the crazy one. For the first time in my life, I did not have to ask Alec or Jeff or Michele what was happening, what the reality was, and how I should be reacting or feeling about it. I had begun answering my own questions.

After 2 months of paranoid, defensive and occasionally irrational behavior on her part, Johanna relieved me of my duties. It was badly done. I was escorted, *escorted,* the 7 feet from my desk to the door. The hurt was enormous, the humiliation profound.

But I was free.

I drove directly to the holistic health center where Michele worked part time at the desk and where I sat for an hour and a half sipping hibiscus tea sorting through my shock. The second person I contacted was my mother.

There was a time in my life when I would have dreaded that call. There was a time when my mother would have assumed that I had blundered; she would have mistrusted my assessment of the situation and leapt to conclusions that put me in the wrong. She would have spoken out of fear for my future, distress over any financial demands my dilemma might make on her, and the infantilizing effect it might have on me. She would have spoken from a midpoint between guilt and glowering, pursed lip displeasure over the fact that I had not measured up to any of her expectations.

Not this time. This time, she was all sympathy. She did not

question that Johanna had been difficult and unfair. She praised me for sticking with it for as long as I did. She told me to be strong.

Something had happened to my mother 5 years earlier. Something wonderful. She had turned into a Mom.

I can tell you the exact moment it happened. She called one morning moments after I had glanced at my sick cat and experienced my first glimpse of the possibility that she might die. At the sound of my mother's voice, I burst into tears and said, "But she is so dear to me!"

My mother answered instantly, "Oh honey, you've got to let her go!"

To my recollection, it was the first time my mother had ever called me honey. And in her voice, there was only love. Nothing else, no judgment or commentary and most amazing of all, no dismissal or renunciation of my tears. It was the first of now innumerable "who arc you and what have you done with my mother?" moments. She bore me up from that moment on.

She had just turned 80 years old.

20
Stone Angels

T HE IMAGERY in "The Hound of Heaven" stayed with me. I liked the idea of God pursuing me instead of the other way around. It increased the likelihood that any synchronicities or epiphanies I might be experiencing were issuing from an authentic Source. I hadn't gone looking for it. *It* had found me.

I have had numerous epiphanies in my lifetime. I have felt supported by actual angels, who I believe are possible even in a godless universe. An angel is a vestigial spark or footprint of a human life that needs only initiative in order to exist and through a prodigious reorganization of energy, can speak to us through our still, small voices, our visions or other human beings.

One day, after spending a morning in the ER with tachycardia, I went downstairs to Cardio-Rehab looking for encouragement from Jeff and Casey. The workout room was crowded and my visible angels were unavailable. One of the regulars—a most elderly man who had never spoken to me before and never spoke to me again—hobbled by and tossed these words in my direction, words I desperately needed to hear at that moment: "God is looking out for you, missy, don't you think He's not."

My most impressive revelation occurred on the eve of my 53rd birthday. I was just slipping into bed and I don't recall thinking anything in particular, certainly nothing of significance, when suddenly I felt—attended.

I leaned in to the sensation and then shrugged. It was that Man at My Elbow, to the right of me and just a little bit behind, Jesus. I had grown accustomed to his comings and goings and I was still pretty much ignoring him.

Then suddenly I—realized? Imagined? Perceived?—we were not alone. Directly behind me stood two strapping angels, heroic figures I knew instantly as St. Michael and St. George. They looked resplendent in their gold plate and gilded wings, warrior angels clasping in the manner of medieval knights unsleeping swords. They had my back.

My cat Taliesin, all black and silky fur, lay draped around my shoulders as she used to, purring, keeping me warm and comforted while I sat writing at my desk.

Just ahead, to the left of me, my father stood with my Grandpa Howe. They were engrossed in conversation, Gramps, puffing thoughtfully at his pipe, Dad waving his arms in his best declamatory manner. They struck me as guides more than guardians, concerned that I should make appropriate choices and uphold their most treasured values, the ones they had risked their lives to maintain.

Behind them standing in a row were my two grandmothers, my Grandfather Moravec, who died when I was 2, and all my deceased uncles. I hadn't yet lost any aunts. They chatted amiably amongst themselves and seemed to be getting on with their "lives" and commitments, one of which was to care about me.

Behind my grandparents stood their parents and extended family. *Their* parents and family stood behind *them*. A great crowd took shape. Suddenly there were thousands fanning back toward a distant, ancient horizon. Ancestors. I knew that even when I could no longer see their bobbing heads, bobbing because they were straining up over each other's heads to catch a glimpse of me, they continued fanning back to the beginning of my line.

Thomas called it a communion of saints and did not doubt them.

When I asked Alec what he thought it was, he stared intently at me for nearly a minute and then just said, "A gift."

I have carried this multitude inside me ever since, and I hold the vision dear even if the only thing it proves is wise Martha's understanding that everyday Martha needs all the help she can get.

I had some hard times after losing my job, even after establishing my eligibility for state-subsidized health insurance and unemployment compensation sufficient to pay the bills (just barely).

My age, my size, and my health doomed me in a competitive job market where employers directed applicants to "dazzle us with your cover letter." The future looked bleak. At times, I saw no future at all. I stumbled backward into a black hole that had nothing to do with the void and everything to do with survival. If I couldn't make a living, I should have to stop living altogether, and when my mood turned hopeless and possibly suicidal, I called Brian, my suicide prevention buddy from work. Who better than him to assess my risk and talk me down? He stayed on the phone with me for 2 hours.

While waiting for time to lift the shock and the pall, I eliminated two courses of action: sliding backward and standing still. That left one other: moving on. Despite the depression and the rage, humiliation, and brutal sense of failure, losing my job presented me with an opportunity. A most opportune opportunity. And one that I had wished for.

It was now or not at all. I could spend just as much time trying to become a published author as a communications coordinator or marketing specialist. Once again I found myself at a turning point asking: if all I want to be is a writer, why bother with anything else?

But that meant—losing weight. It meant—exposure. It meant—taking responsibility. And being less afraid. It meant stepping into my own shoes, easing into my own skin and being the sole rescuer of the possibilities in my life.

I went to work. When I wasn't job hunting, I rewrote *The Odd Body Vanity Squad* for the fifteenth time and rewrote Book Two of *The Secret Name of God*. For both novels, I revised the query letters and all the synopses, the one-pagers, the five-pagers and chapter outlines. I caught up on my diary, started framing my next book, a memoir, and researching the one after that, a historical novel. I resolved to overhaul and complete the five musicals. I touched up and rounded out proposals for the next eight books.

I acquainted myself with the fundamentals of an author platform, of pitches and online professional networking. I studied the book biz in trade publications, literary journals, professional groups and forums, and the proliferating blogs of agents, publishers, social media consultants, and flourishing and fledgling writers. I figured out the uses and usage of Facebook, LinkedIn, and Twitter. (This was before Pinterest, Google Plus, Instagram, and Vine, etc.) I decided YouTube would have to wait until I had lost that hundred pounds.

I sat and stared at the screen a full hour before sending out my first Facebook post. Stage fright, pure and simple.

I battled multiple anxiety attacks as I developed an author website with a professional web designer, which my mother paid for out of Aunt Martha's estate. I started a blog. Initially, I felt the shock of exposure, the stark-naked feel of putting myself "out there," stating *Here I Am*, this is what I know, this is what I want, this is me. But the website and the blog were necessary and, not incidentally, two more items on my wish list crossed off.

I started sending out queries. And got nothing but rejections.

At this same time, I was receiving a steady stream of thumbs-down letters and emails from prospective employers. One interviewer, the director of a funeral home looking for an office manager, told me that he had heard from 120 applicants and planned to interview 60. The receptionist at the state unemployment agency advised me that an ad for an administrative position in town had drawn 2,000 responses.

The odds were worse in publishing and more heartbreaking. Since most queries were done through email now, rejections could be quick. My record time for receiving a rejection from an agent after sending out a query was a minute and a half.

This was a time when every article about the state of the publishing industry began with the caveat that nothing was certain anymore and only one thing was predictable: change. We were told it was the best of times to be a writer because technology was poised to eliminate the gatekeepers and middlemen: agents, editors, publishers, publicists, and legitimate reviewers. We were also told it was the worst of times because now everyone could be a writer, anyone could publish, which raised issues around quality control and the sheer number of players on the stage.

Too many of us wanted the same thing, to quit our day jobs and live the writer's life. It didn't matter that I had wanted it since I was 9; so did at least half the people I read about. Consequently, in addition to spectacular marketing and social media management skills, the aspiring author's most crucial competence was the ability to stand out. Anyone with anything to say had better do it memorably in 60 seconds flat.

Agents and editors sought the fiction writer who could create a *compelling* author brand, an *eye-catching* query letter, an *irresistible* pitch, a *mesmerizing* voice, *quirky, unforgettable* characters, a *thrilling* plot with a *fresh twist*, a commercial premise that would *captivate* the imagination and a sales hook that would make the publishing world *sit up and take notice* and extol his or her book as *the next big thing,* if not the Grail of publishing: *the new Harry Potter.*

Sometimes it wore me out just reading the adjectives for what was expected of me.

Dickens today would be writing *Super-Sized Expectations* and ditching any silly notions he might be having about sentiment, social reform, and redemption. I cannot tell you how tired I became of reading the words "dark," "edgy," and "dystopian" as desirable qualities in a book. It became disturbing after a while. One agent specified the sort of manuscript he wanted to see landing on his desk or inbox as, "Dark, dark, dark. The darker the better."

Sometimes I wept when I considered how out-of-sync I felt.

The odds seemed insurmountable but at least I was free—living ecstatically as a writer—free, until the benefits expired.

Congress, in response to a still teetering economy, had already extended my unemployment compensation by 7 months. It wasn't going to do it again. With my stomach in knots, I called my mother. After 2 stressful weeks of negotiations, she agreed to keep me afloat until my luck changed. Apparently Aunt Martha's estate was more substantial than I had thought. My mother's monthly check would support me, just barely, and only because her one stipulation was that I file for bankruptcy to eliminate my credit card debt.

The gift even greater than the money was her moral support. This was the new Mom. This was my Mom. She offered no words of blame or shame, incrimination or reproach, only an outpour of sympathy and encouragement that I savored as an expression of faith in me. She was glad she was in a position to help.

I lost count of the "who are you and what have you done with my mother?" moments. My heart brimmed up and over when her monthly check came enclosed in a greeting card that showed a worried-looking tiger cub clinging to a tree limb. The words "Hang in there!" were answered by the caption inside, "I'm here for you!" Sometimes the check came with a chocolate candy wrapper that said: "Be free. Be happy. Be you."

I will never know what turned her. I can only say that at this point in my life, I knew a thing or two about priorities changing as we age.

And then, the inevitable. Since my job loss, we had been talking casually about me relocating to Pittsburgh or her to Brattleboro but neither one of us could imagine leaving our situations. All of a sudden she announced that she was ready to let go of her health club, doctors, church community, volunteer activities, family roots, proximity to my brother Joe's second home in Ligonier, Pennsylvania, and vigorous cultural life in Pittsburgh to "join forces" with me in Vermont. We would live together. She would pay the bills and I would care for her in her declining years.

Occasionally the old Mom resurfaced. I started looking at condos, apartments, retirement communities, and adult living accommodations. By the time she arrived for a Christmas visit, I had amassed a quantity of brochures and appointments with landlords but she discarded half of them at once with the reminder that we would be on a strict budget.

Foolishly I had been imagining a spacious rented house or some fabulous retirement community with full service fine dining, a pool maintained at 89 degrees for therapeutic purposes, cocktail hour, and 24-hour concierge service. One evening, after our tour of a particularly dismal retirement facility where we would have shared a one-bath, one-and-a-half bedroom space with linoleum floors and aluminum trim, I asked, "Mom, when you were my age, would you have wanted to move into that sort of situation with your mother?"

In a brief return of old Mom, she pursed her lips and gave me a hard look. "When I was your age," she said, "I had a husband, a house, a job, a pension plan, and savings. You are scarcely in a position to bargain."

The truth of this, the mortification of it, hit me so hard that all I could do was go to another room and sit in long-faced silence until the nausea passed.

All my life, the thought of moving in with my aged mother had ranked second only to bagladydom as the least desirable way of ending it. I had feared devolving into the cliché of the spinster daughter who becomes the caretaker of the elderly parent because her own life has fizzled. It was a worse prospect than Joe's vision for my "nice little life" as an office manager. I experienced some bleak moments that Christmas with the apprehension that all my nightmares seemed to be coming true and none of my dreams.

On the other hand, when finally faced with it, the thought of "joining forces" with my mother warmed me. It felt sweet. It felt right. She was good company. She was my Mom. She was a wise woman, a fearless, exuberant soul with an inquiring appetite for life. We would have wonderful conversations about politics, philosophy, theology, current events, movies, music, articles, and books. We would cook clean, healthy meals together. Go to the pool together. And take walks after dinner.

She would grip my arm and lean in. Just as she had helped me take my first steps, I would support her aged frame as we walked and consider without hysterics or blame what a disappointment we had been to each other, she with her mixed messages and sins of omission, I with my failure to produce grandchildren, to honor and sustain the genes and genealogy of her kind.

In the evening I would sit with her and feel the history behind her, the spread and propagation of our ancestors, the ordeal and rare courage of her generation, the human interest of her own one story. I would reflect on the life lived before I knew her and the things I had seen her do: from gutting and dressing a fresh-killed chicken to looking glamorous in fancy dress at the Kennedy inauguration; from piling her mentally challenged patients into a van and bringing them home for lunch to visit our latest litter of kittens to spending her twenty-sixth wedding anniversary convincing my father to attend porn films in the city's red light district before coming home and swing dancing in the living room; from exploring Machu Picchu and taking a lover at age 78 to outliving everyone else in her line.

She knew me first, she knew me longest. I would sit in the evening and find a deep peace in the bond between mother and daughter, the one and only, once-in-a-lifetime, now and forever bond between my mother and me.

It would be a privilege to share her last days with her. When she went back to Pittsburgh after Christmas, she left me with instructions to continue looking for an inexpensive situation in which we'd be able to co-exist.

What I did for the next 5 months was weep. Alec suggested that I was mourning her death in advance. I was accustomed to weeping, but this was a deep, straight-up-from-the-gut sobbing, a surge of unspeakable love and loss.

"Mommy? What happens to people when they die?"

"Well, they go away and they never come back."

I did most of my sobbing in my car, driving around from appointments to workouts to errands, usually with some unbearably poignant movie score playing in the background.

"They never come back?"

"No. Never."

I considered my mother's life, what I knew of it, wishing I knew more.

"Never, never, never?"

"No. Never."

I thought of Mommy in the prime of life, tucking me in, reading poems that would haunt me forever, like Eugene Fields' tale of a toy dog and tin soldier, playthings that will stand and wait for Little Boy Blue, who has died in the night, to return until they themselves crumble to dust. I wept defenseless tears for a once beautiful, vital, adventurous woman and for a long, lucky life now coming to its end. She was the one now dying, she was the one who would go away and never ever come back.

> And they wonder, as waiting the long years through
> In the dust of that little chair,
> What has become of our Little Boy Blue,
> Since he kissed them and put them there.

It hurt, it hurt terribly, but I knew I was doing the right thing, coping at last with my instinct to equate life with loss, my sad predisposition to experience authentic life only in the fear and loathing of indigestible death.

This was the business of radical transformation, determining my own feelings and how I expressed them. The panic I experienced as a child ill equipped to deal with the vast, breathtaking loneliness of dying, the pain that had to be numbed, had come into its own. I was feeling it now, feeling it full on in all its fury and assuming the responsibility to live with it, not eat it or smoke it, anesthetize it or choke it back down, while trusting that in the midst of overwhelming grief, or perhaps a moment after, there can be joy.

I thought of Alec's words: "You've got to let the mother go."

In the end, she decided to stay in Pittsburgh. She wanted to age in place. She loved it there and her roots were there, but she did not expect me to displace myself. My monthly checks continued. Another item on my wish list had materialized. Freedom.

At around this time, my mother told me that she did not believe in God, not really —the Holy Spirit, maybe, the Holy Spirit made a weird kind of sense—but not God and that she did not believe in life after death.

After a lifetime of hurtful things said and not said, this was the most hurtful remark of all. I couldn't bear the thought of my mother believing that she will dissolve into nothing as though she had never been. Was she not afraid? What could I say to console her or make the prospect less bleak?

All I really had was a poem that she herself had written when she was 71. It's called "Stone Angels." It seems an improvement over people going away and never coming back.

In the midst of life, we are in Death,
We strut our hour upon the stage,
Busy about so many things,
While He waits patiently—in the wings.

And we may choose—
Put blinders on
Or somehow find the grace
To turn and see Him face to face.

I choose to walk the graveyard lawn
To feel the evening coming on,
I touch the angels made of stone
And think of those who are long gone.

Here's Mary Ann from Ireland come,
And Martha, dark-eyed and sure,
There's lovely, fragile Emily
And after her comes me.

And after me, there's mine and theirs,
A lengthening human chain,
Reminding me that through the pain,
Life is not—and never was—in vain.

21
Magnificent Obesity

IN OUR TEENS AND TWENTIES, many of us equated turning 30 with selling out. We defined adulthood as conforming to the world and then screwing it up and so imagined marking our thirtieth birthdays with black crepe. (On my thirtieth, my bar buddies threw me the best surprise party ever.) Next came 40, widely regarded as the dividing line between young blood and the soon-to-be-dead. For a woman especially, turning 40 meant forfeiting one's desirability, fertility, and relevance. (I threw myself a huge party and ordered a sheet cake topped by decorative organza butterflies and the words "Life Begins.")

Fifty is a real milestone because more than half your life is over and you can't escape reflecting on what you've done and still must do or would rather be doing if the universe would allow it. This is when people feel most inclined to hire a Life Strategies Coach, a Creativity Instigator or a Transformation Expert to help with reinventing their lives. Me? I had a versatile therapist.

I had found each decade birthday to be surprisingly painless, which meant that nothing, but nothing, had prepared me for 60.

I recall the summer in my early twenties when cashiers and people behind counters started calling me ma'am. I was no longer miss. Yes ma'am. Thank you, ma'am. The transit from miss to ma'am in one summer felt a little wistful, even fearful, but mostly I felt grown-up and grand.

The latter end of life tells a different story. I was 58. I went to the movies one night and requested a ticket. The young woman in the ticket booth looked me over and asked, "Adult?" I stared at her uncomprehendingly. The friend I was with exclaimed, "Oh how funny, she thinks you're a child!" That didn't make sense either. Then it dawned on me. The young woman, *teenager*, in the ticket booth wanted to know if I was requesting a ticket for an adult or a senior citizen.

I can't even tell you what movie I saw that night. I was so stunned that all I could do was sit bug-eyed and bruised and watch my whole life flash before me, accelerate, crash, and burn.

As I approached my sixtieth birthday, I grasped that by no stretch of the imagination could I ever again refer to myself as young. I could dress, talk, act young, even try to look young, but no amount of evasive action could save me from the reality of turning 60. It was a brick wall dead ahead with no room for swerving. In a rare surrender to the inevitable, I succumbed to a drooping physical sensation and nagging notion that something on a fundamental level, something to an irreversible degree, something momentous, felt spent. There was no more youth in me.

A month or so prior to my sixtieth birthday, I started discussing with friends the best way for us to observe the occasion. This was the new gang that had recently regenerated out of an old gang from colleagues at SIT. The jaunt to Paris was out. The luxury spa week at Canyon Ranch, the cottage on the coast of Maine, even dinner at the Four Columns Inn, were all outlandish notions because neither I nor any of my friends could afford it. As if I needed it, our slender options served as a reminder that my life was nowhere near what I had imagined it would be at this point.

One day over lunch with Mary, I said, "I just don't want to wake up on the morning of my sixtieth birthday feeling like the world's biggest loser. I want to spring up and say, Joy, joy! New world, new life, new me!"

Mary thought for a minute, then said, "Here's an idea. Are you ready for crazy?"

"Crazy? Yeah. Sure."

"We'll be having a party, right?"

"Right."

"We'll probably be at Michele's, right? She lives down by the river."

"Yeah, so?"

"A baptism."

I liked it. Technically, baptism is a rite of admission into the Christian community, a matter of dying and rising again with Christ. Not one of the people who would be involved in my birthday celebration had any use for organized religion, so we would have to improvise a broader basis for what we were doing and why. But I liked it. I liked it a lot.

It had been 5½ years since the ER staff at Brattleboro Memorial Hospital loaded me into an ambulance and sent me up to Dartmouth Hitchcock Medical Center with a heart attack. I had worked through an array of difficult experiences: nicotine withdrawal, tobacco cessation and cravings, drug phobias, and medical phobias in addition to my regular phobias, panic attacks, and heightened death anxiety in addition to my usual generalized anxiety, existential angst, involuntary atheism, and sleepless nights, as well as an abyss of submerged grief and a long, unbroken swell of tears.

I had weathered the distresses of aging, a dysfunctional work environment, countless rejection letters from agents and prospective employers, distraught trips to the Emergency Room, a debilitating illness, insulin injections, deprivation diets, attempts to manage my compulsive behavior, particularly around food, excruciating holiday seasons, long-term unemployment, and bankruptcy.

I had borne severe emotional pain, the kaleidoscopic challenges of therapy and strenuous efforts to eliminate or alter the ghosts in my past, the toxic sludge in my gut and grooved tracks in my brain.

To make matters worse, or possibly better, once I regained my footing, I resolved to tell my story, which introduced the most death-defying feat of all: finding my voice. When I finally felt ready to commit to a book and semi-confident that it would not lead back to smoking, two questions arose: what to emphasize and how to end it.

For 5½ years I had believed that I would emerge from my transformational crisis in a consummate state. I would be the strongest steel that had gone through the hottest fire. Sane, satisfied, individuated, whole. I would be a hundred pounds thinner and playing tennis like a pro. I would have lovers again, an agent, and a three-book contract in hand. I would believe in God. I would be phobia-free and financially secure. I would be sexy and savvy, actualized and empowered, master of my fate, goddamnit, captain of my soul.

To these resolutions, Alec always added, "And living in a world where nobody dies."

Even while still in the throes of what I planned to recount, I expected to end the memoir on a note of triumph. Having conquered all my demons and diseases, I would be the mad genius bohemian once more, radiant, fit, and ready to take on the world.

To which Alec would say, "Good luck with that."

And rightfully so. I had not followed my own timeline. It was time to begin the memoir and I was still morbidly obese. I had gained 34 pounds since my stay in the hospital. I was still in a disordered relationship with food and injecting insulin now. Although my cardiac numbers were excellent and my workout routine remained consistent, I suffered from metabolic syndrome, insomnia, sleep apnea, and spinal stenosis, which prevented me from standing for more than 3 minutes at a time or walking more than a city block before having to sit down and ease the pain.

I was bankrupt, still unemployed, and still broke. At age 60. In a tanked economy. I was still unrepresented and unpublished, still phobic, still prone to anxiety attacks and rapid heart rate, still single and still undecided about God.

With all this, however, I couldn't get Alec to feel sorry for me. One day he asked: You have a roof over your head? Yes. Food? Yes. Clothes? Yes, such as they are. You have a good car? Yes. Family? Well—sort of. Then you're all right, he said.

I left that session wondering at Alec's nonchalance over the fact that my life was still a train wreck until I looked up at the clock tower of the Congregational Church across the street and noticed how crystal clear, how sharp and how brilliant it was.

Not much had changed. And yet everything felt different.

And that was why the baptism seemed so right.

Alec must have felt some satisfaction when he saw me comprehending at last that life was not as linear as I had wished, that just as there had never been an ideal, unbroken childhood, there would never be an uninterrupted future. The straight line could be warped at any point by squiggles, curlicues, and illegible scrawl. And that's okay. It's fine. Although I might be frightened or disappointed by the curves, twists, doodles, and jots, I could accept them as natural, inevitable, or God's will and push on, confident that no matter what awaited down the line, even death, I would cope. And endure.

I had received my wake-up call. I had lost my footing and toppled into chaos. I had reached out for all manner of help and been blessed with support, insight, and glints of grace. Now it was time to integrate my insights and blessing into action and bring my awakened self into being by changing the way I related to the world. Lose the weight that had served its purpose and the anxiety that had outlived its value. Make my contribution to my community, the funky, artsy, working town of Brattleboro, and as much of the world outside it as I might reach. I would start with a story.

She was afraid of her own bathtub.

Nothing I had ever written, with the exception of my diary, had derived from personal experience. The musicals and the novels, while drawn from personal feelings and convictions, remained stories about other people living other lives at other times. The memoir would require a different kind of writing and I could have a medium-sized anxiety attack at the mere thought of stepping naked onto the page. I began with blog posts. As I grew more comfortable peeking out from behind characters and plot, standing on an empty ghost lit stage and telling my own story, I felt progressively more able to share a secret I had never let out.

I was fat.

I found myself willing to speak of things that had been tucked away for years and to relate a story that had helped define me.

Ooooh gross, what is it, is it human?

I'm not taking you anywhere looking like that, I'd be ashamed to be seen on the street with you.

I started releasing the shame. I had released so much else over the past 5 years. As I began shaping the tale of my heart attack and subsequent crisis, I realized with a kind of awful joy that the primary issue in all that time, the issue all my life, in fact, and the nerve center of the memoir as well as the linchpin to my recovery, was and always would be one thing: my fat.

With the decision that fat was the lens through which everything else should be viewed came the belief that my obesity—a source of deep, deep shame, the thing I had denied and endeavored to hide even from myself—should be outed at last and embraced and, in that one moment of freeing revelation, called magnificent.

On the evening of my birthday, one perfect day in June, seven of my friends and I went down to the West River. The rays of a golden sunset brushed the tops of our heads as we removed our shoes and waded into the water singing "Down to the River to Pray." (*Who shall wear the starry crown? Good Lord, show me the way.*) We stood ankle deep in a pool closed off from the river by a half circle of boulders and stones.

I remember thinking as we waded into the water that whatever I chose to do with my obesity, whether I chose to keep it and transform my attitude or let go of it and transform my whole self, *this* was the place where my real journey would begin. It was the sad and vulnerable, shamed and defiant, liberated and magnificent leap toward new life.

There is great fun in placing "magnificent" in front of every word. Magnificent Fun. Magnificent Beans. Magnificent Fool. It doesn't confer absolute goodness upon the thing it modifies. I'm not saying that obesity is all good, healthy, or desirable. But placing magnificent in front of anything, including obesity, gives it grandeur. It gives it gravitas. It gives you a dignified, generous place to begin.

While scooping up handfuls of water over my head, each one of my friends spoke briefly about life and rebirth, about the power of self-reflection and the power of love and the good things to come. When the time came for me to speak, I read from John 3:3.

Jesus answered him, "Very truly I tell you, no one can see the kingdom of God without being born from above."

Nicodemus said to him, "How can anyone be born after having grown old? Can one enter a second time into the mother's womb and be born?"

And Jesus said, "Very truly I tell you, no one can enter the kingdom of God without being born of water and Spirit. What is born of the flesh is flesh and what is born of the Spirit is spirit. Do not be astonished that I said to you, 'You must be born from above.' The wind blows where it chooses and you hear the sound of it, but you do not know where it comes from or where it goes."

All my life I had struggled against the fact that we want to *know* but can't. I had insisted on certitude and absolute truth and found myself thrown repeatedly up against the reality that there was no God's-eye view of the cosmos. And even if there were, there would be no way to prove it.

When I say that not much had changed but everything felt different, I mean that I was learning to feel comfortable with ambiguity, willing to live the questions, not the answers, and acquire Keats's "ability to be in uncertainties." I had concluded that while our humanity may rest in our deep hurt, and while our hurt may reside in not knowing, our healing derives from commitment. The opposite of doubt is not faith, but commitment, commitment to giving ourselves over to what we do not understand.

We left the river, my friends and I, bits of stardust, bodies whose atoms began in stars millions of years ago, specks in an inconceivably vast, lonely universe, for dinner at Michele's house. There were balloons, fresh flowers, gifts, and a sparkling tiara, a starry crown, which I was obliged to wear all evening.

The cake had been custom-ordered and expertly decorated. It was chocolate, of course. It depicted the storefront of a local business, Everyone's Books, with its familiar signage, green-and-white striped awning, and book shelving in the window. The cake decorator had filled the window with four of my books, their titles drawn clearly on the covers. You know what a weeper I am, but all that evening I hadn't yet cried. Until I saw that cake.

I wish I could tell you how to create the life you want, how to manifest your passion within, move out of your comfort zone, or get your sexy back. But I would never presume. Baptism is a symbolic burial and resurrection. Whether we are being purified, sanctified, initiated, or named, we lay down our pride and our past.

Baptism means entering into the struggle of humanity with both eyes wide open and the first thing I saw was the challenge of not knowing.

Is my anxiety the neurochemical consequence of oversensitive amygdalae or in the words of theologian Reinhold Niebuhr, "The inevitable spiritual state of man"? I don't know. Is obesity a disorder or a disease? Don't know. Low fat or low carb? Can't say. Where will it end? My life. Yours. Human life. Earth. The universe. Billions of years from now, will I still be conscious somewhere? Don't know.

Who is this man at my elbow, this revelation of unconditional love standing at my side? My imaginary friend? Jesus Christ himself? Or the power of God flowing through me, the energy that in human form creates life for life's sake and asks painful, unanswerable questions? I really do not know.

After cake, we took our coffee and tea to the living room and formed a circle. While rubbing a token to imbue it with their good wishes, each person in turn urged me to let go of my ghosts, my past, and my fears, and visualize my dreams coming true. I had chosen the token on a visit to the Weston Priory a week before. Mary had kindly paid for it. It was a small silver medallion inscribed with Mary Magdalene kneeling and holding out her hands and the motto "She Loves Greatly."

When it came time for me to speak, I said words I had recently encountered, words that I try not to wear out with thinking but just say because when I just say them, they turn radiant inside me and blaze holes through my fear of nonbeing. They are the words of Rabindranath Tagore, the Indian poet and mystic.

"Death is not extinguishing the light.
It is only putting out the lamp because the dawn has come."

As I sat in that circle formed by well-wishing friends, I emptied myself of all things but gratitude, thankfulness not only for that moment but for the fact that my path from heart attack to baptism at age 60 had abounded with helpers and backers, healers, allies, and friends, a concerned and caring circle drawn from the matrix of small town life.

In the end, it came down to people, the angels I could see, people who listened, called back, made time, people who smiled just right at just the right moment, extended themselves, gave of themselves, maintained their sense of humor, withheld their judgment, shared their stories and earned my trust, people who sympathized, empathized, guided, pushed and pulled, and taught.

Taught, above all. Their acts of generosity and acceptance became lessons that still light my way. They taught me that most people just want to be kind and give the best of what they believe they have. When I was most lost, my healers carried on with the navigational power of the North Star and the patience of saints. You could say they were all of them God standing at my side, if you believe in that sort of thing.

Maybe it's time I do.

Afterword

I CONSIDER THIS ENTIRE BOOK an acknowledgement in disguise, an act of gratitude to the family who shaped me, to the mentors and soul mates who shared in my creative life and to the helpers, healers and friends in Brattleboro who saw me through a difficult time.

I still feel a kick in the gut when I remind myself that nothing in life is permanent except change. I feel amazed when I note the changes that have occurred in the two years since my sixtieth birthday. Another gang has broken up. Key people have moved away. Best friends have moved on. And recently, Alec, my therapist and life guide of 20 years, announced his decision to retire.

It appears that I am being alternately shocked and eased into the vantage point Alec has been driving at for years: the autonomy to trust my own judgment, instincts and interpretation of reality and to recognize the humanity and validity of my feelings. He has always insisted that while it is good to have angels, both seen and unseen, mental health resides in my ability to take care of myself; to feel strong and whole, even if there may be only one person standing tall at my side, as long as that one person is me.

New key people have appeared in my life, people who have amazingly rounded off the wish list I compiled on that bleak day at the office, the list that began with a MacBook Pro and concluded with improved health. .

I am forever indebted to my agent, the versatile and irrepressible Dede Cummings, whose insights, dietary advice and moral support have nourished mind, body and self-esteem.

I am deeply grateful to the folks at Hatherleigh Press for their faith in my work and proud to be part of a community with so much commitment to promoting healthy lifestyles, protecting Earth's resources and supporting naturalist John Muir's observation that "when we try to pick out anything by itself, we find it hitched to everything else in the Universe." They are: publisher Andrew Flach, associate publisher Ryan Tumambing and the editorial team of Anna Krusinski and her assistant Ryan Kennedy, who remained both tactful and flexible while keeping me on the straight and narrow.

I would like to add special thanks to my long-distance buddy, writer Grace Peterson, whose encouraging words sustained me as I closed in on completing the book.

The final items on my wish list, to start losing weight and regain my health, began to manifest when I walked into the office of Dr. Samantha K. Eagle, naturopath, nutritionist and owner of Biologic Integrative Healthcare and Wellness Center in Brattleboro, where the staff provides primary care with a focus on Lifestyle Medicine. Within 7 months, utilizing a therapeutic lifestyle program called FirstLine Therapy, I lost 50 pounds and tapered off on my insulin injections until I was able to dispense with needles and flex pens altogether when my blood sugar reached non-diabetic levels.

While the low-glycemic food and supplementation plan prescribed by FirstLine Therapy are important to my success, there is equal if not more efficacy in the weekly weigh-ins and counseling sessions with Dr. Eagle herself. I am experiencing transformation in the glow of her personalized care, extraordinary generosity, high spirits and dedication to the health and well-being of her patients, the community in which she lives and the world in which we all share.

My mother is still with us, still healthy, although as frail as a crackled leaf and depleted of the joy I so cherished in her. It is painful for me, resistant as I am to change, hungry as I am for immortality, intolerant as I am of the fact that one day even the stars will vanish and the whole sky turn black, to hear my mother say that she is ready to die.

The struggle to lose weight, calm down and find God goes on. I continue to absorb the whole world around me, to ache for things that cannot be and to seek a kind of truce and peace in what unalterably is. I try to bear in mind Jeff and Casey's advice that what matters most is not longevity but quality of life. I am striving now to grow up in time to grow old with grace.

MARTHA TODAY.